Vaya con Dios

JERRIE COBB,

SOLO PILOT

Jerrie Cobb

by jerrie cobb

For God, with joy and gratitude.

... in the shadow of your wings I sing for joy.

Psalm 63

Jerrie Cobb, SOLO PILOT

Copyright © 1997 by Jerrie Cobb
All rights reserved

No part of this book may be reproduced or transmitted in any form or by any means, electronic or mechanical, including photocopying, recording, or by any information storage or retrieval system without prior written permission from the author except for the inclusion of brief quotations in a review.

Edited by: Dena Hall
Ruth Lummis

Published by: Jerrie Cobb Foundation, Inc.,

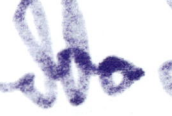

Ruth Lummis
1602 Dower Way
Sun City Ctr., FL 33573-6252

Proceeds from the sale of this book go to help the indigenous people of the Amazon jungle.

Library of Congress Catalog Card Number: 97-92479

ISBN 0-9659924-0-3

First Edition
First printing - September 1997

TABLE OF CONTENTS

Introduction   page 5

Book I: Early Flying Years
  1. Circus Cub To The Great Plains, Part I   9
  2. Circus Cub To The Great Plains, Part II   19
  3. Slow Start To A Dream   31

Book II: Ferrying Fighters, Bombers, Worldwide
  4. T-6 To Lima, Part I   49
  5. T-6 To Lima, Part II   65
  6. B-17 To Paris, Part I   77
  7. B-17 To Paris, Part II   91

Book III: Jack, World's Record, Astronaut?
  8. Jack, Part I   105
  9. Jack, Part II   115
  10. Aero Commander To A World's
      Altitude Record   131
  11. Flight To Space?   143

Book IV: Flying In The Amazon Jungle
  12. Juliet Charlie To Amazonas   163
  13. Juliet Charlie To The Rio Putamayo   179
  14. Juliet Charlie To The Amazon
      Headwaters   193
  15. Shamans Fly To The Moon   207

Index   224

Introduction
by Dena Hall, Editor

This is a true love story. A story of a woman and the world into which she quite literally plunges, a world that swirls around her and beneath her, that loves her, ignores her, breaks her heart, and honors her.

Overlook the pigtails, they will be pulled back into a blond ponytail. Forget the slight stature, she will grow tall. Ignore the lisp, the shyness, she will learn to hide them. Jerrie Cobb becomes a woman and falls in love as a woman falls in love when she climbs into the open cockpit of a 1936 Waco bi-wing airplane. She leaves the earth for the first time and, in a way, forever, never looking back. She is twelve years old.

Determined to devote her life to the sky, Jerrie enters the male domain of aviation by working at small country airports, where she learns the basics of flight and mechanics. She spends the summer of her sixteenth year barnstorming across the Great Plains in a circus Cub. At nineteen she's teaching men to fly. By twenty-one, she's delivering military bombers and fighters around the world, well on her way to becoming one of the world's top pilots.

Never one to go slow, Jerrie falls head-over-heels in love with another pilot, and their romance covers the world.

In her twenties Jerrie sets new world aviation records for speed, distance, and absolute altitude. She is honored by the government of France. Her fellow airmen name her Pilot Of The Year, and award her the Amelia Earhart Gold Medal Of Achievement. She is one of nine women selected by Life Magazine as the "100 most important young people in the United States."

In the infancy of the space age as America begins selecting her first astronauts in 1959, Jerrie is chosen to be the first woman to undergo astronaut testing. Passing the tests with flying colors, Jerrie trains to become the first woman to fly in space. Promising her an early space flight, NASA appoints her a consultant to the space program, but keeps her grounded for three years when politics enters the space race.

In 1963 a Congressional hearing is called for Jerrie to testify on women astronauts. When space hero John Glenn testifies at the hearing that "men go off and fight the wars and fly the airplanes," and women are not astronauts because of our social order, she finds it unbelievable. A few months later, Russia astounds the world by sending the first woman into space, a factory worker named Valentina Tereshkova.

Introduction

Believing that there is much more to life, Jerrie turns her back on fame and fortune when she is thirty-two. Her spiritual adventure leads her to the Amazon jungle of South America where she delights in the challenge of flying over the enormous uncharted jungle, serving the primitive indigenous people.

Fame follows Jerrie as she is honored by South American governments for pioneering new air routes across the Andes, and over the Amazon jungle. President Nixon awards her the Harmon Trophy as the top woman pilot in the world. For her humanitarian work in the Amazon jungle, she is nominated for the Nobel Peace Prize.

Jerrie finds contentment living in the isolation of the jungle, and happiness as she brings seeds, help, and hope to her rain forest friends, while flying in spectacular jungle skies.

This fast-moving dramatic story of one woman's love is told with sensitivity and passion. It is a story of dreams and reality, the constant contrast of the naive child, the innocence, really, with the reality of a perilous life of high adventure in fields dominated by men and politics. In the end, quiet, shy Jerrie is a real "winner" in life.

BOOK I

Early Flying Years

1. **Circus Cub To The Great Plains...Part I**
    Year 1947   Age 16   page 9
    Flying for free, barnstorming
    Dreaming under the stars
    Playing in the clouds

2. **Circus Cub To The Great Plains...Part II**
    Year 1947   Age 16   page 19
    First flight, learning to fly
    WACO bi-plane
    Working at country airports

3. **Slow Start To A Dream**
    Years 1949-1952   Age 18-21   page 31
    Searching for a flying job
    Miami International Airport
    T-6 check-out

CHAPTER 1

Circus Cub To The Great Plains
Part I
Year 1947　　Age 16

"I have this feeling that life is a spiritual adventure, and I want to make mine in the sky."

  The summer of my sixteenth year, life couldn't have been sweeter. On my birthday in March I passed the tests for my pilot's license.
  In May I graduated from high school, after a long struggle. Now it's June, and I'm flying to my heart's content in a faded yellow 1932 Piper Cub. There's nothing like flying to set your spirit free!
  Feeling free as the breeze, I'm thinking this is what life is all about. It's not about money or power or prestige or sex. It's about exploration and adventure and freedom and faith. It's about living with a heart full of joy because the world is so beautiful. We don't need a map for the journey. We only need to wander, and wonder.

Circus Cub To The Great Plains
Part I

The world, the sky, the universe are so exquisite. Flying gives me the freedom to explore. The sky opens to me a world without borders, a life without limits, a universe full of adventure.

Dreaming big and working hard, I've been flying for four years now, and I know there's a great big, wide, wonderful world out there just waiting to be discovered. I feel like the happiest kid in the entire Great Plains, because I can go exploring every long summer's day, from dawn to dusk, in my circus Cub.

It isn't really mine. It belongs to the owner of a little one-elephant circus that tours around the small farm towns of Texas, Oklahoma, and Kansas during the summer months. His name is Mr. O'Reilly, and he agreed to let me fly his Cub all summer long. What a wonderful answer to my dreams, flying for free! Especially for one who has spent all her free time after school, weekends, and every summer for four years working at small country airports to earn short hops around the field. Flying for free is indeed a dream come true!

Well, almost for free. All I had to do was spend four months rebuilding the Cub after its many years of neglect. Now we, my circus Cub and I, are free to spend the summer barnstorming across the prairie, as long as we follow the circus route and do a few fun chores.

Circus Cub To The Great Plains
Part I

Like circling low over farm towns and tossing out the "flyers" announcing the circus coming to town.

Like finding a vacant field near the small towns where we can land, and take the local dignitaries up for rides.

Like paying our own expenses, and keeping the Cub well maintained.

Mr. O'Reilly meets us at each little town and gives me the gasoline to fly the dignitaries. After I've given the courtesy rides, he hands me a box of new circus advertisements, and gives me another five gallons of gas to fly to the next town.

The rest of the time, we can fly as much as I wish as long as I pay for the gas. That's where barnstorming comes in. If I can make enough money giving airplane rides to pay for the gas, we can fly to my heart's content. And that's exactly what we're doing, my circus Cub and I.

What great fun it is! Circling country towns, watching the kids running to catch the circus "flyers" fluttering down to earth. Landing in a farmer's fallow field, or pasture. Taking the mayor, sheriff, school principal, minister, up for rides. And anyone else who has some spare change to help pay for the twenty-cents-a-gallon gas.

Circus Cub To The Great Plains
Part I

The sheriff usually goes up first, just to make sure it's safe for the others.

"You sure you know how to fly this thing? You look awful young to be a pilot. And a girl at that!"

Since I'm not very good with words, I smile and point to the hand-lettered sign I carry in my Cub.

AIRPLANE RIDES
400-hour experienced pilot
$1.00   (kids $.50)

After the town dignitaries have had their free rides, there's usually some other brave souls who will pay a dollar to fly with us, many for their first time aloft. It's a special privilege to take someone up for their very first flight. I try to make it as smooth and calm a flight as possible, so as not to frighten them.

Flying from the rear seat in the tandem Cub, I watch their expressions as they turn to peer out the open door, enjoying the thrill of leaving the ground for the first time.

"Why, just look at those people down there. They look like little ants running around."

"The cars all look like kiddie cars. Even the houses are small."

"Oops. Do you have to put the wing down like that when you turn?"

Circus Cub To The Great Plains
Part I

"There's old Salt Fork Creek. Never knew it meandered around like that."

"Hey, do we have to go back so soon? I'm just getting used to this flying thing. This is fun!"

I'm learning more about flying, and human nature, than I ever dreamed possible. It would make a good theme on "how I spent my summer vacation." But this is not a vacation. It's just the beginning of how I plan to spend the rest of my life. I have this feeling that life is a spiritual journey, and I want to make mine in the sky.

From early morning to late afternoon we are almost always in the sky. Practicing flying maneuvers, tossing out circus leaflets, flying to the next little town, giving rides. There just aren't enough hours in the long summer days, to satisfy my love of flying.

Every time we earn a few dollars giving rides, I buy more gas so we can practice some more. To learn everything about flying that my circus Cub can teach me is my goal.

She's a J-3 model and I have to block her wheels with big rocks before pulling her propeller through by hand to get her engine going. Her engine has forty horsepower which gives us the power to fly almost sixty miles per hour in level flight, a little less in climb, sometimes a little more in a dive. Regular car gas is her nourishment, which I carefully pour into her tank, bucket by bucket.

14 Circus Cub To The Great Plains
Part I

She is simplicity itself. No battery, starter, radios, or lights. Her fuel is measured by a not very accurate piece of cork with a wire through it. Since gravity is what keeps her gas flowing from her one tank to her engine, we can't fly inverted for very long before her engine is starved for fuel.

Her flight manual has long since been lost, so I just keep nudging her flying performance until she shows me in no uncertain terms I've gone too far. Many are the times I scare myself so badly, I have to fly along the straight and narrow for a while to get my courage back. You get acquainted with yourself, really get to know yourself, flying solo in a Cub.

She lives on gas, oil, and constant loving care. I live on Wonder bread, bologna, and a lot of love from the farm families in whose fields we land. They invite me to supper sometimes, serving the freshest vegetables I've ever tasted. Often they invite me to spend the night in their farmhouse, but unless it's raining, I prefer to sleep out under the stars with my circus Cub. Besides, I want to protect her from any stray cows that might wander over to lick the varnish off her fabric with their sandpaper-like tongues.

It's hard to fully appreciate the beauty of the night sky until you're far away from all the lights, trees, and houses. The best view is lying on your back on the open prairie looking straight up. On a

Circus Cub To The Great Plains
Part I

clear night you can see the brilliant stars from one end of the horizon to the other. And the Milky Way with its trillions of stars is directly overhead.

Lying on my bedroll next to my Cub, I wonder at the beauty of the star-filled sky. Face to face with infinity, I dream of spending the rest of my life flying in the boundless sky. Nighttime's my time for dreaming, daytime's my time for doing.

I awake to a day filled with marvelous possibilities, and can hardly wait to climb into my Cub and take off into the gorgeous sky. Summer mornings in the Great Plains are normally clear and crisp. Sometimes, in the purple light of early dawn in the high cold stratosphere, thin cirrus clouds stream across the sky, as if blown by the breath of God.

By noontime the prairie heat is rising, and cumulus clouds start building. In the late afternoon the towering cumulus can become gigantic thunderheads that spawn lightning, heavy rain, hail, and an occasional tornado. From these we keep our distance, knowing my fragile Cub can be destroyed in an instant. When we spot a tornado we fly as fast as we can in the opposite direction.

To flirt with thunderstorms is to expose our frailness to wind shear beyond our structural limits. Heavy rain can quickly drown our little exposed engine. Hail can easily rip the worn fabric from my

Cub's wings and fuselage, leaving us a windblown stream of rubbish across the prairie floor.

But I love to watch the violent storms from a safe distance. Seeing the lightning dance across the vast prairie, especially at night, is a glorious sight to behold. From my bedroll under my Cub's wing I often watch for hours as the lightning keeps the sky aglow, and the ground echoes the thunder's baritone rumblings. It seems like God is speaking in the vastness of the sky, as well as in the still small voice deep within.

In the cool of early morning when the prairie looks so fresh and clean, we practice our flying maneuvers. When the clouds begin forming, we fly off to play among the young stratus and cumulus before they mature in the rising heat of day, and become rain-making factories.

My love affair with clouds began when I was much younger, but now, thanks to my circus Cub, we are able to get within touching distance. Like a blind man feeling the face of a friend, we gently touch all their contours and curves as the clouds begin building, expanding, stretching.

Sweeping, swirling around the billowing clouds, we roll from one steep bank to another, practicing control coordination. What a totally different view of clouds you get from above and among them! Seeing them only from below, one can't begin to know of their magnificence.

Circus Cub To The Great Plains
Part I

Sometimes we try to out-climb a towering cumulus, circling around and around in maximum climb. Usually we lose the game, as the clouds grow faster than we can climb. Admitting defeat, we dive into a narrow "canyon" between two towering clouds, spiraling around one, then the other, all the way back down.

Playing among the hallowed halls of clouds is sheer delight. They are playgrounds in the sky reserved for the fortunate who fly.

Our last flight of the day and first in the morning, at the time of the long shadows, is always special for my Cub and me. Sometimes we do a loop or two, or some slow rolls, just to celebrate the gift of flight.

Within a month I'm changing my sign from 400 to 500 hour experienced pilot, and I'm having as much fun as the kids. I especially like taking them up for their first flight. They are always so excited, taking it all in vividly, and are seldom as scared as their parents. They just can't quit talking about flying, and begging for more, which I usually offer since I'm practicing technique, and building up flying experience.

The kids are ingenious in figuring out ways to earn their fifty cents contribution for gas money.

"Besides my chores at home, I'm going to weed Farmer Blackwell's garden next week so I'll have money for the gas when you come back."

Circus Cub To The Great Plains
Part I

"My birthday's tomorrow, and I'm telling everyone, the only thing I want is more airplane rides, with you."

"I'm planting tomatoes now so I can sell them when they're ripe in August, and have the gas money for my rides when you come back."

"I'm eating lots of watermelons so I can make pickles from the rinds, to sell, so I can fly with you some more."

Boys and girls alike, age five and up, eager to do whatever it takes to earn another flight. They remind me of someone else who did everything she could to learn to fly.

These kids are getting a head start on me. I didn't get my first airplane ride until the relative "old" age of twelve. But there was never, ever, anything I really wanted to do in life more than fly.

CHAPTER 2

Circus Cub To The Great Plains   Part II
Year 1947   Age 16

"As soon as we left the ground, I had the wondrous feeling of being truly free for the first time."

Before my first flight, the freedom of racing a quarter horse across the Texas plains at full gallop, bareback, was the closest I could come to the total freedom I craved. After I tasted the pure delight of the sky, I knew the ground was no longer my home.
From age twelve on there was never any doubt about where I would spend the rest of my life. The sky was the only place I felt really at home. Everywhere else it seemed like I was out of place. Being a pilot had always been my dream. After my first flight, it became my passion.
Born in Oklahoma, I grew up on Army bases during World War II, memorizing silhouette cards of military bombers and fighters. Like the other kids, my sister Carolyn and I were lovingly called "army brats" as we moved from camp to fort, to base, every year or two when Dad was transferred.

20 Circus Cub To The Great Plains
Part II

Never in one place long enough to make close friends, I became somewhat of a loner, finding my fun in solitary and simple pursuits, like cloud watching. And star gazing, as I slept out in the back yard during the summers.

Mother made our home a happy one wherever we were living. Carolyn and I were given a lot of love, and taught discipline, respect for our elders, and that children should be seen and not heard. That was fine with me since I didn't like to talk anyway.

Carolyn was two years older, pretty, and the model child. While she was cutting out paper dolls, I was folding paper gliders. As she listened to Deanna Durbin sing on the radio, I practiced the dots and dashes of Morse Code. We always shared the same room and, like sisters everywhere, sometimes we disagreed. "Why can't I keep my model airplanes on my side of the room? You have your dolls on your side."

Carolyn was always logical. "Because my dolls are pretty, and your airplanes are ugly."

Around age four I remember running after my sister right into the middle of a field full of stickers. My bare feet got so full of stickers I fell, getting stickers in my legs, arms, hands, hair. "Tare, Tare, (I couldn't talk plainly) come help me," I cried.

Circus Cub To The Great Plains
Part II

Carolyn was playing with her older friends in the field, with shoes on, of course. She came over to see what her baby sister wanted.

"You got into that sticker patch because you followed me, after I told you I didn't want you tagging along. You can just sit right there, pull your own stickers out, and find your way back home by yourself. And don't be a crybaby."

It took a long time, but I did pull all my stickers out, stopped crying, and found my own way home. Lessons learned: Don't ever follow anyone. You're on your own. Don't count on anyone to help you out of life's sticker patches. Most of the messes you get into are your own doing anyway. And don't ever cry about it.

Like oil and water, school and I didn't mix well. It started out wrong the very first day, when my kindergarten teacher made fun of my lisp, and all the kids laughed at me. To a bashful five-year old it was devastating.

After two tongue-clipping operations, months of expression lessons, and learning to talk with a "bone" under my tongue, I was finally able to say "three" without a lisp. But the damage was already done. Being tongue-tied, and ridiculed, was too much to handle for a shy little girl.

School never got any better. It became something that had to be endured until I was old enough to fly on my own. My biggest fear was having to repeat a grade, which would just prolong the agony. So I studied hard, and made sure that didn't happen.

My first flight was in 1943 in a bi-wing open cockpit Waco with my dad as pilot. Climbing up on the lower wing and into the rear cockpit was exciting. Looking at all those dials and controls right in front of me was fascinating. Being tightly strapped in with shoulder harness and seat belt, hearing my dad explain the hand signals he would use to communicate with me, was comforting. It seemed like a wonderful dream was coming true.

We taxied out in the little bi-wing, turned to line up with the farmer's field, and suddenly we were airborne. As soon as we left the ground, I had the wondrous feeling of being truly free for the first time. It was the happiest I had ever felt, in all my twelve years. Then my dad gave me the signal to follow through on the controls as we climbed, and turned, and soared, through all that open space up there. I was beside myself with joy.

I loved feeling the freedom of the sky, being able to move in all directions at once, up, down, right, left. Sensing the friendliness of the sky, I felt perfectly attuned to this new environment. It was over with too soon, and we had to return to that ordinary world on the ground.

Circus Cub To The Great Plains
Part II

Dad was stationed at Sheppard Air Field and was building up flying time to get his Army Air Corps wings, which he hoped would lead to an overseas assignment during WWII. I spent the summer camped out by the Waco in the farmer's field outside of Wichita Falls, Texas, learning everything I could about her. And keeping her washed and waxed, always dreaming of my next flight in her.

My dad fastened large blocks on the rudder pedals, and I gathered an assortment of pillows, so I could sit higher in the rear cockpit and see out better. I wanted to see everything there was to see, and feel the wind on my face.

When Mother wondered why I was suddenly so enthusiastic that summer, I overheard my dad say, "It's flying that puts that sparkle in Jerrie's eyes. I hope it never fades."

The days my dad practiced aerobatics were the most fun of all. I couldn't get over all that open space up there, a universe in which to roam. I could see forever, and do anything I wanted to, roll, and loop, and spin, and glide, and float, and spiral. Never did I feel one twinge of fear in the sky, just pure overwhelming joy.

Suddenly it all came to an abrupt end. Dad was transferred to Lowrey Air Field in Colorado, and we had to part with the Waco. Brokenhearted is too mild a word for a twelve-year-old who has lost her first love.

Circus Cub To The Great Plains
Part II

Once again I retreated into my private world. For my dad, flying was a means to an end. For me, it was my whole life. I had to find a way to fly, no matter what it took.

Wherever we were stationed, I began going to the public library and checking out every book that had anything to do with aviation, reading them over and over again at night. After school and weekends I bicycled out to small country airports. At first I would hide behind a tree or sign, and consider it a privilege just to watch the flying activity from a distance.

The biggest obstacle to my flying was my shyness. At age twelve and thirteen it was downright painful to talk with strangers. Or to answer questions like, "Why are you hiding behind that tree?"

Eventually some very kind mom-and-pop airport operators invited me in, and shared their love of aviation with a bashful young girl who wanted to fly more than anything else in the world. The pilots of the small airplanes would give me a ride around the field in exchange for the odd jobs they found for me to do.

My favorite job was washing the airplanes, for then I could become familiar with every nook and cranny of the airplane, and study how the air flows over the wing and tail surfaces to create lift. Cleaning the oil and exhaust smoke off the belly of the light planes was fun too, because I had to lie

Circus Cub To The Great Plains
Part II

under the airplane belly, an excellent position to avoid talking, and watch the little airplanes making lazy circles in the sky.

From under the airplane I could also study the technique of every takeoff and landing. Lying on my back with my arms reaching up to scrub the soot off the airplane's belly with gasoline-soaked rags, I often became distracted watching the planes in the air. It didn't take long before the rags would drip gas, running down my hands to my elbows, and into my armpits, burning, and bringing me back to reality with a start.

My reward came late in the day. A trip around the field in the sparkling clean airplane I had spent all day washing and waxing. Sometimes my reward could stretch into twenty or thirty minutes of wonderful instruction by the owner-pilots of the small airplanes, who loved to fly as much as I did.

I was enthralled with flying, and became a real hustler to learn everything I could about airplanes, mechanics, navigation, meteorology, and civil air regulations. Eagerly volunteering to serve as a mechanic's helper, gas girl, and all-around small airport "gofer" helped me learn about engines, airframes, maintenance, and repairs.

After four years of working at small airports after school, weekends, and summer vacations, I was fortunate to accumulate more than 400 hours of flying time, in a variety of small airplanes. But I

Circus Cub To The Great Plains
Part II

had to wait until my sixteenth birthday to take my first pilot's test.

At one of the country airports where I worked for flying time, the mom of the family operation popped popcorn on Sunday afternoons for the pilots sitting around "hangar flying." After thinking about it for weeks I got up my nerve one bright Sunday afternoon to ask about an old, neglected, yellow Piper Cub sitting out in the weeds.

Sam, one of the old-time pilots, answered.

"Pitiful, isn't it? Letting a plane run down like that. Belongs to a fellow name of Wally O'Reilly. He used to fly it around the Great Plains dropping leaflets over the small towns advertising his circus. He got so busy keeping his little circus going, it hasn't been flown in years."

After thinking a bit, he added: "That's what you need. Something like that to practice your flying in."

"Boy, that would be my dream come true," I blurted out without even thinking. "But I'd have to work ten years for the money to rent her, and then I'd be too old to fly."

"Listen to her. Sounds like an old lady. How old are you now? Fifteen? Sixteen? Didn't you just pass the test for your pilot's license?"

The airport mom saw my face starting to blush, so she kindly answered for me. "Yes, but Jerrie plans to be a professional pilot, and that only gives her two more years to study, and practice for

Circus Cub To The Great Plains
Part II

her Commercial Pilot's tests on her eighteenth birthday. She also plans to get her Instrument, Multi-Engine, Flight Instructor, and Ground Instructor Ratings. And her Airline Transport License when she's old enough."

Harvey, the airport mechanic, chimed in with a grin: "Bet you could pass them all right now if you were just old enough to qualify. But Mom's right, you're going to be busy, no time to waste in non-flying jobs just to rent a broken-down Cub."

"Hey guys," he added, "Why don't we put in a good word for the kid to Wally? Maybe he'd let her fly his Cub this summer. She could drop the leaflets advertising his circus while practicing her flying. And we could all pitch in and help her get the Cub back in flying shape."

They all agreed that would be good for the Cub, good for Wally, and good for me. One of the farmer pilots volunteered, "Wally's coming by my place tonight to pick up some hay for his elephant. I'll mention it to him."

Mr. O'Reilly did agree to let an eager sixteen-year-old girl fly his airplane. And that's how I got to be a flying advance person for a one-elephant circus.

Harvey, Sam, and all the airport "regulars" helped me clean up the circus Cub, patch her up, and get her engine running again. Whenever I needed a repair part to make her airworthy, Mom, Pop, Harvey, Sam, or one of the other pilots miraculously

Circus Cub To The Great Plains
Part II

found an used one that I could clean up, repair, and use, for free.

On the day the Cub and I left for the circus circuit, they gave us a special barnstorming popcorn party. With a purring engine, and a tank full of gas, they waved us off for three wonderful months of flying around the Great Plains. I could hardly see to take off from the small grass field for the grateful tears in my eyes.

My bedroll, water, and gas bucket were strapped to the front seat, a loaf of Wonder bread and a pound of bologna stowed behind the rear seat. With five hard-earned dollars in my pocket and a circus Cub to call my own, I felt like the richest person in the whole wide world.

For the first time in my life, I have the use of a beautiful airplane to teach me about flying, and that's exactly what she's doing. Not a day passes that we don't spend many happy hours together, learning of wind and weather, spirals and spins, maintenance and maps.

At dusk she sets down ever so gently on a farmer's soft field, where I spread my bedroll beside her as we settle in for the night. Sitting under her wing eating my sandwich I'm treated to an almost nightly display of "heat lightning."

Circus Cub To The Great Plains
Part II

Feeling honored to have a front row seat, I watch the marvelous light and sound show of lightning dancing across the prairie horizon backlighting the towering clouds in the distance. Sometimes I watch for hours, captivated by the beauty, and thanking God for the wonder of it all.

I've begun my life's adventure, but my spiritual life isn't exactly growing by leaps and bounds. Easter Day of my twelfth year I was baptized, but like a vaccination I was afraid it didn't take, because nothing was very different. Now I feel a need to learn more about God who is blessing me with this gift of flight. We may be a tiny airplane with one soul on board in the vast prairie sky but we are not alone. He seems a very close and constant companion.

Like flying, there was never a time I remember of not being aware of God. With so much beauty all around, especially in the sky, there just has to be a loving God who created it all. Now I'm an experienced Cub pilot, touring the Great Plains country for the circus. The magnificent sky is my altar, where every lovely hour aloft is filled with the beauty of his creation.

I feel a kindred spirit with a nineteen-year old RAF pilot killed in World War II. He wrote this poem, that was lived by a circus Cub pilot every single day in the summer of her sixteenth year.

Circus Cub To The Great Plains
Part II

HIGH FLIGHT

Oh, I have slipped the surly bonds of earth
    And danced the skies on laughter-silvered wings;
Sunward I've climbed and joined the tumbling mirth
    Of sun-split clouds - and done a hundred things
You have not dreamed of - wheeled and soared and swung
    High in the sunlit silence. Hov'ring there,
I've chased the shouting wind along, and flung
    My eager craft through footless halls of air.
Up, up the long, delirious, burning blue
    I've topped the windswept heights with easy grace
Where never lark, or even eagle flew.
    And, while with silent, lifting mind I've trod
The high untrespassed sanctity of space,
    Put out my hand, and touched the face of God.

                      John Gillespie Magee, Jr.

CHAPTER 3

Slow Start To A Dream
Years 1949-1952   Age 18-21

"Living is full of risks. Sometimes we have to just start out, with nothing to go on but blind faith."

It's a tough time to begin a flying career. But then I guess it's never easy. With World War II ended, thousands of highly experienced military pilots are out looking for the few civilian flying jobs available. Not much chance for an eighteen-year old with a brand new Commercial Pilot's License. Especially a girl.

To hold onto my dream of flying professionally I begin a seemingly endless string of non-flying jobs; waitress, typist, bookkeeper, horse trainer, theater cashier, professional softball player. I take any job I can find to earn the money to live, and continue flying.

Sometimes I work two or three jobs at the same time. Renting airplanes is expensive. To save money I stay in the cheapest rooms, and buy chili for dinner because it comes with free crackers and ketchup to make it go farther.

Every free hour is spent around local airports, doing any odd jobs just to be around airplanes. I especially like helping the mechanics, so I can learn more about repairing airframes and engines.

My birthdays continue to be celebrated with a new pilot's license or rating as I reach the minimum age. Now I'm a Commercial Pilot and a Certified Flight Instructor. Also, I have Certified Ground Instructor Ratings in Civil Air Regulations, Navigation, Meteorology, Airframe and Engines. But I have no flying job.

Occasionally I find fill-in work in low paying flying jobs, like pipeline patrol, crop dusting, flight and ground instructing, but they are always part-time or temporary, until a "real pilot" (male) can be hired. It gets pretty discouraging.

While reading the help-wanted classified ads in the aviation newspaper "Trade-A-Plane," I come across one ad that might have possibilities: "New airline seeks DC-3 co-pilots willing to work for experience only."

Since most professional pilots expect to get paid for flying, I wonder if I might have a chance for this non-paying job. Flying as co-pilot on the legendary DC-3 would be great experience, and I'd be grateful to have any flying job. I could find another job during my off-duty time to pay for rent and food.

Slow Start To A Dream

Too shy to call the number listed, I send a telegram listing my qualifications. For days I anxiously wait, finally an answer arrives. Yes, they will consider me for an interview, if I come to their office in Florida, at my own expense. With glee I throw my things into my old Pontiac and leave immediately to drive straight through to Miami, 1800 miles from Oklahoma.

One thing I failed to mention in my telegram was my gender. When they notice I'm not of the desired sex, even the non-paying job evaporates. The interviewer says, "We can't expect our passengers to fly with a girl co-pilot. Why, they're already scared of flying, and a girl in the cockpit will frighten them even more. You may have all the licenses and ratings in the world, and ten million hours of flying experience, but no airline passenger will ever fly with a woman in the cockpit."

As an afterthought he adds, "If you really want to fly, try the stewardess office down the hall."

Rejected and dejected, I drive around Perimeter Road to the end of runway 9L at Miami International Airport. Shedding a few private tears, I wonder if I will ever find a real flying job.

Before long the sights, sounds, and smells of the busy airport soothe my disappointment. Just being able to see the big airplanes, hear their engines roar, smell their burned fuel, cheers me up and gives me hope that I'll be in a cockpit again soon.

As darkness closes in, I'm enchanted by the colored lights of the big airport all lit up at night. Blue taxi lights, white runway lights, red caution lights, white rotating beacon. It's like a big fairyland, and I want so much to be a part of it. I know my dreams are big, but I'm willing to work hard and take the necessary risks to help make them come true.

It's exciting looking around the tropical sky full of stars, for the lights that flash, signaling the white strobe lights of an airliner coming in to land. Thinking of everything that's going on in the cockpit, I call off an imaginary check list as the pilot lines up his airplane for final approach.

Sitting on the hood of my car at the end of the long runway I keep my eyes glued on the big plane as it stays right in the center of the glide path all the way down. Goose bumps pop out all over me as the plane comes roaring over, just a few feet above my head, to a perfect landing on the runway just ahead of me.

All the lights and activity of the big airport so captivate me that I stay the night watching the big airplanes land and take off. And wondering if I will ever be a part of this wonderful scene.

By morning it's foggy and not many airplanes landing, so I go over to Jerry's Cafe on LeJuene Road. Seated at the counter, I order a cup of chili, and eavesdrop for hours listening to the pilots who fly the big airplanes talk flying.

Slow Start To A Dream

Without enough money to buy the gas to drive back to Oklahoma, and willing to take any job just to be around airplanes, I drive around Miami International Airport looking for work. That's when I spy a small sign reading:

Minimum wage openings:
Mail Clerk   Typist/File Clerk
Apprentice Mechanic   Janitor

Before I lose my nerve, I run right in and apply for the apprentice mechanic slot. They say they can't consider a girl for the mechanic's job, but they offer me the typist/file clerk position. Since I know aviation terms they put me to work in the hangar, typing up work orders on airplanes. It's not flying, but it's a job. And it's on a big airport ... in a hangar ... surrounded by airplanes. Things are looking up.

About six months later, while walking around the hangar early one morning I hear some shouting out on the ramp.

"What do you mean, you won't fix my airplane without a work order? I didn't fly all night just to be held up by some dumb paperwork. I want it fixed now, and I want it fixed right."

The man shouting is a pilot who has just landed in Miami, and is trying to get the brakes fixed on the Peruvian Air Force T-6 he is flying. The lead mechanic on the graveyard shift answers, with equal intensity. "Those are the rules around here. We can't touch an airplane without a work order. And the office doesn't open for two more hours, 0800.

"Wait a sec. There comes the girl now. If you're nice to her, maybe she'll cut you a work order early."

The pilot turns to look where the mechanic is pointing. "You mean that kid? The blond girl? She does the work orders?"

"Yeah. She's crazy about airplanes. Comes in early every morning just to look at the planes we're working on. She doesn't start work for another two hours, but you can ask her."

The pilot starts walking toward me, saying, "Hey, Miss, the mechanic won't fix my airplane without a work order, and he says you're the one to ask."

Pointing to his airplane leaking hydraulic fluid on the ramp, he continues.

"That T-6 was due in Peru last week, and I can't get it to Lima without brakes or hydraulic fluid. It's costing me $100 per day penalty until I get the Commanding General's signature on the dotted line as delivered to the Peruvian Air Force in Lima. Can you help me out?"

Always glad to help, especially another pilot, I answer. "Sure. Sounds urgent. I'll unlock the office for that. Come on in, and give me the details for the work order."

Slow Start To A Dream

A few minutes later the mechanic has the work order, and tows the T-6 into the hangar. Feeling better now, with his airplane getting some attention, the pilot asks, "How about a cup of coffee? I'm buying."

That's how it happens that I'm sitting in a small airport coffee shop at Miami International Airport at dawn, listening to exotic tales of ferry pilots delivering airplanes all over the world.

It's Jack Ford talking, legendary pilot, WWII hero. "After the excitement of wartime flying, I opted for the adventurous life of an international ferry pilot. Started my own company, call it Fleetway International. We're a prime contractor to the U.S. Air Force, under the Lend-Lease Program, and keep about forty pilots busy delivering surplus military planes to foreign governments around the world. Sometimes we stay on after delivery to set up training programs for the foreign military pilots.

"Usually it's more fun than this T-6 contract. And these penalties are costing me my shirt. Not only are they doing a lousy job of overhauling them up in New Jersey, but my big, strong, macho pilots are afraid to fly them. They'll fly broken-down bombers anywhere in the world. But just mention single-engine over ocean and Andes mountains, and the sissies start making excuses. So, here I am, trying to deliver the first one, and looking around for some other good pilots."

I almost choke on my coffee.

Did he just say "looking around for some other pilots?" The words my ears most want to hear? Before I can get scared, I blurt out, in almost a whisper, "I'll fly your airplanes to Peru."

Jack has the same occupational problem of many longtime pilots, a slight hearing loss.

"What? Did you say something?"

With all the nerve I can muster, I stammer out, a little louder. "Yes ... I'll ... I'll fly your T-6s ... to Peru."

Jack replies with a laugh. "Ha, a girl, a kid yet! You some kind of student pilot?" "Forget it! I don't have time for wanna-be pilots."

Remembering his manners, he adds, "But I wish you well."

With another laugh. "Give me a call when you get a couple of thousand hours under your belt."

Embarrassed and tongue-tied again, I can see my dream job vanishing fast. The only thing I can think of to do is pull out my wallet of pilot credentials, and spread them on the table between the cups. While Jack politely glances at them, my voice returns to add, "My log book contains 3,161 hours and 25 minutes certified flying time, in forty-one different airplanes."

Jack looks me in the eyes, smiling, and shaking his head. "Well, what do you know! It looks like you really are a pilot. My apologies. I didn't think you were old enough to have all those licenses, ratings, and flying time."

He hesitates a few seconds, then adds. "Maybe I should give you a try. I'm really in a bind right now with these T-6s coming off the line."

I can almost see him thinking out loud. After another pause, he continues. "You want a flying job? O.K., I'll give you a try. But fair warning, it's dirty, it's difficult, and it's dangerous. Nothing "glamorous" about it. I doubt you can handle it. Ever fly a T-6?"

My courage comes back as the subject moves to flying. "No sir, but I'll learn fast."

Jack pays for the coffee while I gather up my licenses and wait for him at the door. On the way back to the hangar, I'm ecstatic, almost walking on air, as Jack rambles on.

"I want you to know the job is temporary. Only until I can shame some of my hotshot pilots into flying these T-6s to Peru. Hopefully they're smart enough to figure out that if a girl can do it, a kid at that, maybe they can."

That's fine with me. I'm just happy to get any flying job. And I'm used to taking the jobs the guys don't want. At least Jack is up front about it.

He continues, "While they're working on my plane today, I'll hop an airline up to New York, train over to Trenton, and pick up another T-6 for you to fly. Meet me here on the ramp at 0530 tomorrow. I'll check you out in the T-6, then we'll head south. Got a passport?"

I'm sure glad I'd planned ahead, and used my first paycheck to get a passport, just in case I ever had a chance to fly overseas.

"Yes sir, a brand new one, never used."

"Good. You'll need to buy some khakis. Gotta fly in uniform."

With a wave, Jack is gone, just like Santa Claus.

I stand there in a daze, wondering if I have really been offered my flying dream job. In hopes that my dreams are finally coming true, I start getting ready.

After catching up on all the work orders, I explain to my boss that I have to quit my job as typist/file clerk because I've been offered a flying job. Driving to the local army-navy surplus store, I cash my paycheck, and buy two pairs of khaki slacks and two khaki shirts.

Then I drive to my rented room, load all my stuff into my car, and drive down to the Coral Gables library. There I spend the rest of the afternoon looking up the North American T-6 in "Jane's All the World Aircraft" and "Warplanes of World War II." I make notes, study the specifications, and try to memorize all the performance data that I can find on the T-6.

When the library closes I drive back to the airport and park in the maintenance parking lot. Then I begin learning everything I can about the actual airplane. Walking around Jack's repaired T-6 on the ramp makes my heart beat faster at just the thought of getting to fly a big, powerful military airplane.

North American Aviation manufactured the T-6 as an advanced trainer, nicknamed the "Texan," during World War II. This model T-6G has been converted to a fighter with the addition of fifty caliber machine guns, and bomb racks under the wings. It has the radial Pratt and Whitney 1340 engine which develops 650 horsepower. Just looking at that big round engine with all that power makes me quiver with excitement.

The rest of the night I spend sitting in the cockpit of Jack's T-6, memorizing everything I can about her ... where the important instruments and gauges are located, flaps and gear levers, speeds, power settings, radio frequencies. And thanking God for this beautiful answer to my dream.

The dozens of non-flying jobs I had to take just to stay in aviation fade into insignificance before this one great opportunity.

Beside myself with joy, surrounded by all the twinkling lights of the international airport, sitting in the cockpit of my first "big" airplane, my first military fighter, I can hardly wait for the sunrise. It's hard to believe that in just a few hours I'll be flying an airplane three times more powerful than any airplane I've ever flown before. To Peru.

A man of his word, Jack lands in Miami early, at 0445, after flying all night again. He taxies to the ramp, motions me into the rear cockpit of the T-6 without shutting down the engine. I'm sure glad I memorized where things are located. The little red lights glow only on the instrument panel, and I forgot to bring my flashlight.

Jack's B-4 bag occupies the metal bucket seat, and since there is no other place to stow it, I sit on top of it. I can see out the sides, but have no forward visibility, except the dark outline of Jack's head and shoulders in the front cockpit.

By sliding down farther on the lumpy B-4 bag in the seat, I can just barely reach the big rudder pedals with the tips of my toes. It sort of reminds me of a twelve-year-old who had struggled to reach the controls, and see out of an old bi-wing Waco.

Jack taps his head with his hands cupped over his ears indicating I should put on the earphones. I find the headset by tracing the cord with my hands in the dark, and slip it over my ears, adjusting the microphone close to my lips. Jack is all business, as his deep voice booms in my ears on the intercom channel.

"I know you can't see out very well from back there, so I'll taxi out. Be sure to strap in tight, with your shoulder harness locked into your seat strap."

Slow Start To A Dream

I feel in the dark for the shoulder harness and seat strap, finally getting them locked together. While he taxies out, Jack continues briefing me on the intercom.

"With that big engine up front you'll have a lot of torque on takeoff, so stay on those rudders. Don't let her even begin to get off the center line, or she'll ground loop faster than I can say 'cat'.

"O.K. now, you're lined up on runway 9L. The tower has cleared us for take off. She's all yours. Go."

I have never considered myself a brave person. Sitting there in the dark cockpit ... at the end of the well-lit runway ... at the controls of the most powerful airplane I have ever been in ... I'm about to run out of courage.

Peering into the dark night at the big airport lit with fairyland lamps, I know I have to do it. Even if I die trying.

Knowing better than to ask, but wondering how I am going to keep the airplane on the runway center line when I can't even see it, I cautiously start the throttle up slowly. That's when I feel Jack slam his throttle wide open, and suddenly we're careening down the runway behind 650 wild horses!

His voice is strong on the intercom.

"Stay on those rudders ... more.

"Stick forward, just enough to lift the tail.

"Keep her straight ... walk those rudders.

"Stick back, ease her off now.

"Level off, just above the runway.
"Gear up, let her speed build up.
"Establish climb.
"Ease the flaps up.

Thankful to be safely in the air, my legs are still shaking, when Jack comes back on the intercom.

"O.K. Circle back, and try a landing.

"And if you don't stay on those rudders, you're going to have a basket case.

"Downwind, slow her down ... more.
"Gear down, locked.
"Base leg, partial flaps.
"Turn final, tower's cleared you to land.
"Check gear down, locked.
"Full flaps, prop forward.
"Slow her down ...nose up.
"Hold her off ... off ... off.
"Three point, oops, you almost lost her there."

Jack taxies the T-6 back to the ramp. I feel like a total failure, knowing I would have lost this powerful airplane had Jack not been there to correct my mistakes.

Doing my best to hold back the tears, I know I've just lost the most perfect flying job I could ever imagine. Jack is right. I can't handle it. I'm lucky to be alive.

Taxiing in, Jack continues on the intercom.

"I know you can't see over the nose from back there. With a parachute and life raft under you, and some pillows, you'll do fine from the front cockpit. You've got to have full travel on those rudder pedals. All in all, not too bad ... for a kid."

My emotions take a roller coaster ride, soaring from rock bottom to the stars. Jack is still going to let me fly this T-6 ... to Peru!

He continues briefing me on the intercom. "The narrow landing gear gives the T-6 a built-in ground loop. And with the torque from that big engine up front, it takes a lot of rudder control to keep her straight on the runway. Once she starts, she'll whip around so fast you won't know what happened. She's a bear on the ground, but a gentle bird in the air. You'll like her."

Before I can ask, Jack answers.

"There's no time for another circuit now. I'll have to talk you through the next few takeoffs and landings by radio, until you get the hang of it.

"You go find some pillows, and supervise the refueling. I'll check weather, and file our flight plan. We'll be off for Camaguey, Cuba, at sunrise."

Wow! Just like that. I'm leaving on my flying dream job after all. The only problem is, I'll be flying solo in a powerful airplane that I've just demonstrated I can't handle.

I begin to rationalize. Living is full of risks. Sometimes we have to just start out, with nothing to go on but blind faith ... even if it does seem foolish ... and is frightening.

Scared as I am, I'm not about to say "no" to my dream coming true.

Here is Miss Jerry Cobb, a former Aerodex employee, with Jack Ford, President of Fleetway, Inc. Jerry, who has many hours in the air, is flying this AT-6 to Lima, Peru.

BOOK II

Ferrying Fighters, Bombers, Worldwide

4. T-6 To Lima...Part I
    Year 1952   Age 21   page 49
        Start, take-off, formation flying
        Cuba, Jamaica
        Colombia, ground loop

5. T-6 To Lima...Part II
    Year 1952   Age 21   page 65
        Arrested in Ecuador
        Military prison
        Peru

6. B-17 To Paris...Part I
    Year 1953   Age 22   page 77
        Coby, snowy take-off
        Long legs on the North Atlantic
        Greenland

7. B-17 To Paris...Part II
    Year 1953   Age 22   page 91
        Almost mid-air collision
        Narssarssuaq Air Base
        Paris, DC-3 to Miami

CHAPTER 4

T-6 To Lima   Part I
Year 1952....Age 21

"This is it. Do it, do it right, or die trying."

Jack is in a hurry. Jack always seems to be in a hurry. But at $100. per day penalty, perhaps he has good reason to be in a hurry.

The gas truck is still pumping fuel into our airplanes when he returns.

"Weather's good, flight plan's filed. Let's get those tanks topped off, and be on our way. Did you find some cushions?"

Jack completes the refueling while I run over to my car in the maintenance parking lot and grab some old pillows. He crawls into his T-6, waves, and hollers, "Let's get going."

I climb into the front cockpit of my T-6, and strap into the bucket seat tight, sitting on top of my parachute with a one-man life raft beneath it. So tight that I can't reach the brakes on top of the rudder pedals. With a little loosening, and the pillows doubled behind me, I'm finally ready to taxi.

Sitting alone in the cockpit of my T-6 staring at all those gauges, instruments, bomb and gun sights, about to take-off on a long ferry flight over ocean and mountains, is scary. But there isn't time to even think about it.

Jack has taxied out, and I'm left sitting on the ramp, searching frantically for the starter switch. Nowhere, among all the dials and switches can I find anything that even faintly resembles a starter button.

The baritone voice is on the intercom.

"What's the matter, Cobb? We're been cleared into position for takeoff as a formation of two Peruvian Air Force airplanes. I'm in position on the active runway, and you're nowhere in sight. WHERE ARE YOU?"

"Sorry, sir, but I'm still on the ramp. I've looked everywhere but I can't seem to find the starter switch."

Hoping he'll forgive my stupidity, if I find an excuse, I add, "When you checked me out in the dark this morning, you never shut down the engine, so I didn't learn how to start a T-6."

By the time Jack cancels our take-off clearance, taxis all the way back to the ramp, shuts down his engine, unbuckles and climbs out of his T-6, strides across the ramp and jumps up on the wing of my parked T-6, he hasn't cooled down a bit. He slams my canopy back, hangs his head into my cockpit, right next to my left ear, and bellows.

"See that energizer pedal in full view on the floor, between the rudder pedals? Hold that down with your heel until she's cranked up. Then go forward with your toe. Prime, throttle, mixture.

"Catch her right off, or you'll have a ball of fire shooting out the exhaust that'll singe your hair. If that doesn't work, you'll have to hand crank her, and that can break your arm. So catch her the first time."

Energizer pedal? That's a new term to me. Hand crank a 650 horsepower engine? Sounds a bit like starting an over-powered Model T Ford.

By doing exactly as Jack directs, my guardian angel sees to it that all 650 horses roar to life the first time, and we taxi out for take-off.

Cleared into position to hold, we sit at the end of runway 9R at Miami International Airport. My T-6 is tucked in just behind the left wing of Jack's airplane, ready for my first formation take-off. At least Jack is ready. I'm so scared my legs are shaking on the rudder pedals, as I talk to myself.

What am I doing here? About to take off solo in the most powerful airplane I've ever flown, a military fighter I almost crashed an hour ago.

I start a pep talk again. Sure it's risky, but so is living. To live we risk dying, to try we risk failing, if we never risk anything we'll never do anything.

The tower clearance booms in my headset.

"FAP 552 formation, cleared for take-off, right turn after take-off. Climb on course."

This is it. Do it, do it right, or die trying. You're on your own now, no one to take over if you lose control.

A puff of black smoke coming out the exhaust of Jack's engine signals that he has fire-walled his throttle. Taking a deep breath, I do the same, with more bravado than I really feel.

Concentrating mightily, playing the rudder pedals, weaving from one side of the runway to the other, suddenly we are airborne, with little help from me.

It isn't exactly a clean formation take-off, but we are safely in the air. I'm still alive. It's a gorgeous day. "Thank you, God."

Looking out on the emerald islands of the Florida Keys surrounded by the turquoise waters of Florida bay is a beautiful sight. The lighter blue of the Gulf Stream river running through the darker blues of the Caribbean sea is fascinating. But sightseeing will have to wait.

There's a world of difference in visibility between the front and rear cockpits of a T-6, especially in the air. With my parachute and life raft under me in the bucket seat, and the pillows behind me, I can see out fine now. But I can't see Jack's T-6 anywhere in the sky.

T-6 To Lima   Part I

Just as my legs are beginning to stop shaking, his voice comes through my earphones. "Are you lost again, Cobb? You're supposed to be flying my left wing position. Heading one-five-six degrees. Between Key Biscayne and Bimini Island."

Quickly turning to one-five-six degrees on the compass, I finally spy his airplane, way ahead and off to my left. "Roger. I'm a little behind you, catching up now," I radio, trying to sound casual, as I open my throttle to maximum power.

A few minutes later I shoot by Jack's T-6 like it's standing still in mid air. Embarrassingly I admit, "I've never flown formation before. Guess I need a little practice to get the hang of it."

But I don't. The harder I try, the worse I get. Circling back, adding power to catch up, climbing, diving, I'm all over the sky. No matter what I do, I'm usually lost way behind Jack's T-6. Or whizzing right past him, as he just stares incomprehensibly.

Jack is back on the radio.

"How in the world did you ever manage to fly over 3,000 hours, and never learn formation flying? Oh, I forgot. You were always flying those little 'puddle-jumpers.' You have a lot to learn, kid."

Since I'm trying with all my heart to be a "big airplane" pilot, I decide to ignore that radio contact. Finally, Jack starts coaching.

"Fall back.
"Come up slowly. SLOWLY.
"Decrease throttle BEFORE you pass by.
"Bring her in closer.
"You're too high, too fast, too far out.
"There you go again, right on by"

Formation flying looks so easy. But it's proving to be beyond my competence. It's a relief when Jack radios. "At this rate you'll be out of fuel half-way to Cuba. Tell you what. I'll give you headings which I expect you to fly within two degrees. I'll fall back, and fly YOUR wing position. You just hold her straight and level, on course, 65% power, 7,000 feet altitude."

With that, Jack makes a beautiful peel-off, a steep climbing turn, then comes around and tucks his plane in to stay, right between the left wing and fuselage of my T-6. Just like that! Close. Closer than I have ever been to another airplane in the air.

Jack's T-6 is so close I can see the whiskers on his unshaven face. And I can't miss the big grin spread across his face, as he has so effortlessly shown me how a real fighter jockey flies. He's back to business on the radio.

"You're off your heading. Turn back to one-five-four degrees now. I expect you to hold it right on. Your altitude too, within fifty feet."

Intent on keeping my exact heading and altitude, I barely glimpse the coast of Cuba as we pass over. Soon it will be time to land this "bear," and we aren't even acquainted yet.

Jack is coaching again.

"In military fighters we make a 360 degree overhead approach for landing. I'll handle the radio communications with Camaguey tower. You do exactly as I say. Since you can't fly formation, I'll have to follow you in. I'll be right behind your left wing, so if you ground loop, I'll have to also."

It isn't bad enough that I might crash one airplane. Now, if I can't land safely, two airplanes are at risk.

Alone and frightened, my total concentration is on flying the airplane, and Jack's words.

"Upwind, head for the center of the airport.

"Let your speed build up, you'll need it later.

"Start a dive, down to 400 feet.

"Right over the runway, to the middle.

"Now, sharp pull-up.

"Start a steep climbing turn to your left, forty-five degree bank.

"Bring her on around.

"Reduce power.

"Gear down, locked.

"Keep her turning.

"Slow her down.

"Full flaps.

"Roll out, now.

"Check gear down, locked,
"Keep her straight.
"Hold her off, off, until a full stall.
"Walk those rudders."

By the grace of God, we're down safely. With two bounces, but no groundloop.

Jack comes back on the radio. "Not too bad for a learner. Next time get your control stick ALL the way back."

Taxiing is getting easier, even with wobbly knees. But I can't understand why two Cuban soldiers are standing at attention on the ramp, saluting. I keep looking around to see who they are saluting.

Jack comes bounding up on my wing, shoving my canopy open. "As a military aircraft commander you now carry the rank of Captain. You'd better return their salute, or they'll be standing there all day."

Loosely, half-waving, I do my best to return their salute, with shaking hands. Jack doesn't approve. "You'll have to do better than that, if you're going to fly Air Force equipment."

A fast refueling, and we're off for Jamaica. My T-6 doesn't frighten me quite so much now, but we're a long way from being friends.

Landing in Kingston just before dark, I learn we never leave our airplanes overnight without refueling, no matter how tired we are. Jack explains.

T-6 To Lima   Part I

"In the tropics condensation will cause water droplets to form on the inside of metal wing tanks that aren't full. Over the ocean is no place to find out that your engine won't run on watered-down gas."

After clearing customs and immigration, checking in with airport administration, refueling, and the long drive into the city, it's after nine before we arrive at our "crew" hotel, the old South Camp Road Guest House. For the first time since yesterday the thought of food enters my mind, and I discover I'm famished. Over a late supper, Jack briefs me on tomorrow's flights.

"Wake up call at 0400. Leave for the airport at 0430. Top off the tanks again because they settle overnight, and we'll need every ounce we can cram in during the morning cool."

"Take-off at sunrise, around 0600. Kingston to Barranquilla, Colombia, a long leg, right on the maximum range of the T-6. All ocean, not even a reef in between to check course or winds.

"At best, we'll have a twenty minute fuel reserve, so pray we hit the coast right at Barranquilla, and for good weather. The tropical trade winds are right on our nose, if they're as much as five knots stronger than predicted, we'll be swimming. Better get some sleep. Good night."

It still seems like a fairy tale come true. I'm in Kingston, Jamaica, having survived two solo take-offs and landings in a military T-6 that I'm flying to Lima, Peru.

My mind is full of so many things I want to savor. I walk through the hotel gardens, smell the sweet jasmine, look at the tropical sky, listen to the faint strains of calypso in the distance. A rooster crows.

It's after midnight when I return to my small room, sit on the bed, and sew the Fleetway wings Jack gave me, onto my khaki uniform shirt.

At 0430 I meet Jack on the front steps and crawl into the waiting taxi for the long ride back to the Kingston International Airport. Ferry pilots don't eat breakfast, I find out. Restaurants are not usually open at four or five in the morning when we're heading to the airport.

Ferry pilots don't eat lunch either, since we're flying all day. Smart ferry pilots carry tins of tuna, spam, sardines, in their B-4 bag I learn, as Jack tosses a tuna tin over to me while I'm pre-flighting my T-6. "Here, you might get hungry before we find Barranquilla." Fortunately he has taped a small G.I. can opener onto the top of the tin.

After topping off the tanks again, we're airborne a little after six, climbing toward the rising sun. Maybe my leg muscles are getting stronger. My T-6 doesn't seem to wobble so much on take-off this time.

Jack still has to fly my wing position, because we need every ounce of gas just to make it to South America. There's none to spare for my futile attempts at formation flying.

Concentrating on keeping the exact headings and altitude doesn't leave much time for looking around. Nor do I dare take my hands off the controls to open the tuna tin.

There isn't much to see anyway. Hundreds of miles of southern Caribbean ocean with nothing but angry waves kicked up by the strong tropical trade winds.

The range of our T-6s is four-hours to dry tanks. Our flight plan calls for three hours and forty minutes. We have been flying over three hours without a single check-point to verify our position, winds, or speed. Now we're well past our point of no return, and are committed to make Barranquilla, or land short in the ocean. There are no other choices.

With about thirty minutes of fuel remaining, and the fuel gauges nearing zero, my low-frequency radio suddenly finds a signal strong enough to home on. It's sure a welcome sight to watch the ADF needle swing straight up, indicating the BAQ nondirectional radio beacon straight ahead. For the first time in a long time Jack's mike button clicks.

"You're getting better at holding a steady course. You now know Barranquilla is dead ahead. But how far? Can we make it?"

Looking ahead through the haze for the South American coast reveals nothing but more ocean. While I'm pondering the answer to his question, Jack continues on the radio.

"If you look straight down you'll see a line in the water separating the muddy brown water from the blue-green of the Caribbean. That's caused by the Magdalena River draining the northern half of Colombia, and dumping her muddy water into the Caribbean at Barranquilla. It takes about 40 miles before the Caribbean can absorb all that mud."

"We are within forty miles of the coast so you can start a gradual descent now. You'll see the coastline in about fifteen minutes. Just beyond, you'll find Soledad airport down the river and on your right."

Jack talks me through another landing, and I'm beginning to say nice things to my "bear." She hardly even wiggles off the center line.

After a fast refueling in the heat and desert wind of the northern coast of South America, we're off again on the next leg to Cali, Colombia. What a welcome change, flying over land!

Following the Magdalena River valley through northern Colombia we're treated to beautiful scenery of verdant green hills, floodplain, and foothills of the Andes. There are check-points, landmarks, radio stations, all along the route, to check our ground speed, navigation, and winds. I feel spoiled.

T-6 To Lima   Part I

It's late afternoon when we arrive over Cali after a beautiful flight. Jack decides he'll land first this time, to check the runway. He makes a beautiful peel-off to the left, and I follow him around.

Rolling out on short final, I watch the whole thing as if in slow motion. Just after touch down, Jack's T-6 veers right, then a hard left, spinning off the runway into the grass. Burying the left wingtip in the hard ground, washing out the left gear.

I reach for the throttle to make a go-around but decide it's not necessary since the runway is clear. Landing short, I taxi around some big holes in the runway up to where Jack is just climbing out of his ground-looped T-6. Shutting down right on the runway, I run over to find Jack unhurt, leaning on the left wing of his wounded "bear." He's talking to himself, wondering how and why he ever got involved in this Peruvian Air Force T-6 program.

Crash wagons appear, and after much discussion about the damaged landing gear and wing, Jack supervises the lifting of his T-6 onto a makeshift tow dolly. He rides in the back of the tow truck watching his bent airplane, while I taxi my T-6 into the ramp.

There we learn it will take approximately six weeks, Latin America time, to repair his airplane. He isn't in a very good mood. "What do you mean, seis SEMANAS (six weeks)? Seis DIAS (six days) would be more like it!"

To which the head mechanic replies.

"Capitàn, the wing is broke. Needs much repairs. And the landing gear maybe broke too. Six weeks fast for major airplane repair."

Jack is angry, with himself, and the head mechanic. "You have two mechanics, tools, and materials here at 0700 tomorrow. I'll show you how to repair it in seis DIAS. If I have to fly with the landing gear BOLTED down, I'm leaving here inside of a week."

Later that night, at our crew hotel in Cali, Jack tells me what happened. "Tower cleared us to land. They never even mentioned they'd been working on the runway. The workers left in such a hurry at four, they didn't bother to mark the big holes they had been cleaning out to repair.

"The Tower never received our flight plan from Barranquilla, so they weren't expecting incoming traffic. Of course I have to hit one of the holes on the right side, which tosses us into a deeper one on the left, then throws us out into the grass.

"No major damage, except maybe the gear. A lot of sheet metal work on the wing repair, probably take a week or so, the way they work around here, in between siestas."

T-6 To Lima   Part I   63

I assume Jack will take my T-6 on to Lima, so I ask. "May I stay here, and help with the repair? I learned a little about sheet metal work growing up around local airports. That way I can guard your T-6 at night too, by sleeping in her, and make sure she's ready when you come back."

For the first time all day, Jack smiles.

"No, I thought about that, but fair is fair. I dinged my "bear," I'll stay and fix her up.

"You're taking off at 0600 tomorrow for Guayaquil, Ecuador. Then Peru, Lord willing. And get the General's signature on that piece of paper to stop the $100 a day penalty."

My "bear" and I did eventually make it to Lima, but not before being arrested and put in a military prison in Ecuador. But that's another story.

CHAPTER 5

T-6 To Lima   Part II
Year 1952   Age 21

"Maybe solitude is not a goal, but a path. Without freedom it doesn't serve."

"You come to bomb us. You go to prison."

"No, sir. I don't want to bomb anybody. There are no bombs in those racks under the wing."

I have just landed in Guayaquil, Ecuador, taxied to the ramp, and shut down my T-6 in front of the tower. About forty armed soldiers rush to surround my "bear" and me. I push my canopy back and step out on the wing, smiling. That's when the soldiers yank me to the ground and push my face into the hot asphalt. One of the soldiers keeps his heavy boot on the back of my neck while the others tie my hands behind my back. By pulling on the other end of the rope, they force me to my knees on the hot ramp.

"You bomb the frontier with Peru. Admit it. We find out."

"No, sir. I come from Cali, Colombia, not Peru. Please check my flight plan, with the tower."

"You lie. The tower receive no flight plan on you. Peru send you to bomb us."

"You have my passport, all the official papers on the airplane. Look at the landing permit from the Embassy of Ecuador in Washington. It says your government granted permission for this airplane to land and refuel in Guayaquil, en route to Peru."

"That was before we have war with Peru. Where you shoot guns? Drop bombs?"

"Nowhere. There are no bullets for those guns. No bombs. Look in the ammunition compartments, they are empty."

The hot asphalt of the ramp is burning my knees through my khakis, and sweat is rolling down my face from the hot sun. Finally I'm allowed to stand. Then the soldiers prod me with the bayonets tied onto their guns, forcing me into a small room below the tower.

Seated in a straight back chair with my hands still tied behind my back, I'm forced to sit very uncomfortably on the front edge of the chair. Their commandante continues his interrogation.

"You are Peruvian spy. You come to bomb Ecuador. Tell me truth."

"No, sir. I am a North American ferry pilot, delivering the airplane to the Peruvian Air Force."

"See, you say it. You fly for Peru Air Force. You come to kill Ecuadorians."

"No, no, no. I don't want to kill anybody. I just want to deliver the airplane to Peru."

Things are going from bad to worse. From the one window in the small room I can see the soldiers swarming all over my T-6, opening up all her compartments and inspection plates. They are going through my maps, knapsack, scattering my personal effects over the dirty ramp, taking my camera.

My interrogation at the airport goes on for hours. Every few minutes more high ranking officers from the Ecuadorian military arrive to see the "blond Peruvian Air Force girl spy pilot" they have captured.

Towards evening a General of the Ecuadorian Air Force arrives from the capital, Quito, to continue the interrogation. With a room full of soldiers carrying bayoneted guns, and me rather skinny at 110 pounds, he decides I'm no longer a threat to anyone, and orders my hands untied. Then he tries to make friends.

"You can talk to me. I will help you. Tell me truth. How long you work for Peru Air Force?"

"But, sir, I do not work for the Peruvian Air Force. I work for a U. S. company called Fleetway International. I am a North American ferry pilot delivering the airplane to Peru."

"I cannot help you if you do not tell me truth. We know you are a Peruvian spy. They send you here to bomb us. You must admit everything."

"You don't understand, sir. I am a North American citizen. You have my U. S. passport. I don't speak Spanish, how can I be a Peruvian spy?"

"You are imposter. Peru give you counterfeit passport, dye your hair, send you to Ecuador to kill our people. Entiende Español bien (you understand Spanish well)."

The General obviously doesn't believe me. They load me into a Jeep, and drive to the prison at their military base.

The saddest part is having to leave my "bear" in their custody, sitting on the hot ramp with all her compartments open. And it's starting to rain.

At the military prison barracks there is a another problem. Since they have never had a woman prisoner before, they don't know what to do with me. To put me in the main barracks with all the men prisoners doesn't seem right.

After much scurrying around, I'm led into a small room near the barracks entrance. It had been the prison guard's room, and he isn't very happy at being moved out to sleep on the front steps. The soldiers push me into the tiny room, slam the door, and lock it with a large padlock.

More interrogations follow each day. The pieces of the puzzle are finally coming together. It appears that sometime after the Ecuadorian Embassy in Washington granted permission for my T-6 to land and refuel in Ecuador en route to Peru, the two countries began fighting over their common border.

Like children playing tit for tat, Peru captured some Ecuadorian soldiers in the "no man's land" they both claim on the frontier. Then Ecuador captured some Peruvian soldiers.

The only refinery making aviation fuel is on the Peruvian side at Talara, and now Peru has refused to sell any avgas to Ecuador. The entire Ecuadorian Air Force is grounded for lack of fuel.

In the middle of this crisis, comes a Peruvian T-6G with fifty caliber machine guns, and bomb racks under her wings. The fighter is painted in the bright blue and yellow of the Peruvian Air Force, with the Peruvian flag proudly displayed on the tail. And it's flown by a solo girl pilot, wanting to refuel in order to fly to Peru. Their attitude is becoming more understandable to me.

With Jack's T-6 down in Cali for repairs, and mine now confiscated by the Ecuadorian military, we're batting zero.

When Jack gets word of what is happening in Ecuador, he immediately hops an airline out of Cali for Miami, and another to Washington. His contacts in the State Department start sending cables to the

United States Embassy in Quito asking them to do everything in their power to get us released.

At least it gets me an English speaking person to talk to. A representative from the U.S. Embassy in Quito arrives at my prison barracks on the fourth day of my captivity.

He announces he is here only because his bosses in Washington insisted. That he has left the high, cool air of Quito and flown down to the steamy coast just to visit me. He adds that he detests the heat and humidity of Guayaquil, and he can hardly wait to return to cool, dry, Quito within the hour.

He proceeds to give me a lesson on the rights of U.S. citizens in foreign countries. Basically, it boils down to zero. He says I am jailed under the laws of Ecuador, and the U. S. Embassy can do nothing to help me.

When I ask him what laws of Ecuador I have broken, and what charges are against me, he says he doesn't know exactly, but rambles on to say I'm in a lot of trouble. Because I was caught as a spy flying a Peruvian Air Force airplane, under the Peruvian flag, they will probably lock me away for years. Or at least until the war with Peru is over.

Figuring that I'm not going to get any help from him, I hurriedly write a note for him to telex to Jack at the State Department in Washington, D.C.

"You told me the U. S. Air Force is giving this T-6 to Peru under the Lend-Lease Program for $1.00 per year, and paying for it's delivery to Peru.

Technically the airplane should still belong to the United States until safely delivered to Peru by a U.S. pilot, and the $1.00 lease payment is paid. If the Ecuadorian military thinks they are holding U. S. property illegally, they just might release us."

It's worth a try. Being a prisoner in a military prison in Ecuador is not part of the flight plan for my life.

After a week with no word from Jack or the Embassy, I'm getting discouraged ... and hungry. The watery soup they serve the prisoners twice a day is not something I can drink much of. When it becomes noticeable to the guards that I'm losing more weight, they start bringing me rice with a gruel over it. That solves the food problem. I eat it.

A seaport on the equator, Guayaquil is hot and humid, in the 90s on both counts. My only clothes are what I had on when they arrested me. Fortunately I was wearing a T-shirt under my khaki shirt, so at least I have something to mop up my sweat.

I scratch marks on the wall to keep track of the days, just like in the movies. I sit cross-legged on the iron cot when I'm not pacing the three small steps of my room for exercise. The worry, the boredom, the depression is getting to me. What if I'm stuck here for years like the Embassy man said? What will I do?

I have to find some way to work at something. I can't just lie around doing nothing all day. Work is needful for the soul, as well as the mind and body.

What will I read? I'd better start learning Spanish right now. It was my foreign language in high school, but I wasn't very good at it. After three years of studying Spanish in school I could conjugate verbs, but not speak a single coherent sentence.

No one in the prison speaks any English so I begin learning Spanish in a hurry whenever I'm allowed out of my small room to the exercise yard. My fellow prisoners and guards catch on fast to the point and mimic method, and seem more than happy to teach me their language.

What is my family thinking? They will never understand why I have to spend the best years of my life in an Ecuadorian military prison.

I lie awake a lot at night looking at the tropical sky through my one barred window, thinking. About God. About family, friends. About the sky. About flying. I think about all that I love, how everything I treasure is really a gift from God.

Ever since I can remember, I've been somewhat of a loner, enjoying my time alone. Now I'm alone, and not enjoying a minute of it. Maybe solitude is not a goal, but a path. Without freedom it doesn't serve.

T-6 To Lima   Part II   73

One night, while watching the profusion of stars in the equatorial sky through my tiny window, I suddenly know I will be back in the sky again soon.

Two days later, with no explanation, I'm given my passport back, loaded into a Jeep and taken to the airport.

What a beautiful sight, my T-6 unharmed, unguarded, and all buttoned up! My clothes and camera have been thrown back into my knapsack, and put in the rear cockpit seat. Somehow, they even found some avgas to top off her wing tanks.

Quickly I check her over, jump into the cockpit, crank her up, and taxi as fast as we can to the end of the runway. It's late in the day to be leaving, but I want to get across the border before the Ecuadorian military change their minds. After thirteen days of being held in prison as a Peruvian spy, the relative safety of Peru sounds like paradise.

In the last rays of daylight, just as the sun dips into the Pacific, we cross the border and land safely on the shell runway in Talara, Peru. "Thank you, God."

At the small guest house on the beach I luxuriate in the one outdoor shower, washing the dust, dirt, and sweat of thirteen days in military prison into the ocean. A cold saltwater shower never felt so good. And clean clothes are a downright luxury. There's even fish for dinner. Life is good!

After a good night's rest we take off at sunrise, following the coastline south, with the majestic Andes mountains on our left, the deep blue Pacific Ocean on our right. It feels so good to be back in the sky! We swoop down and play with the waves. Then pull up and flirt with the mountains in the early morning light, happy to be back in our element.

This is what I missed so terribly. The freedom of the sky, and being surrounded by the beauty of God's creation.

After flying the long legs down the Peruvian coast my "bear" and I have become friends. Late in the day, with the sun low over the Pacific, we land at the military air base in Lima.

The Peruvian Air Force knows all about our troubles in Ecuador, and has it's marching band playing as they welcome us with open arms. We are among friends.

CHAPTER 6

B-17 To Paris   Part I
Year 1953   Age 22

*"We can't always have life the way we want it.
If we always have to wait until we're ready,
we'll miss out on a lot."*

She sits on the ramp in the freezing rain. The legendary B-17 of World War II fame. I would be happy merely to see her, touch her, ride in her. I am being given the privilege of flying her. To Paris.
We first meet late in the dark winter day. I recognize her immediately from the silhouette cards I studied as a child. Never even dreaming I would ever be flying a B-17.
The famous Flying Fortress that World War II pilots said always got them home during the war, no matter how badly she was shot up. The song, "Coming In On A Wing And A Prayer," was written for her.
She will be the first four-engine bomber I've ever flown. My first ferry flight across the North Atlantic. My first trip to Paris. Wow!

Just back from my seventeenth ferry flight to South America, the freezing weather at Westover Air Force Base is a shock. Dropping my B-4 bag, parachute bag, and over-water gear bag by her nose wheel, I pull out a heavy sweater to ward off the cold. But I can't keep from walking around her, admiring her lines, she fascinates me so.

Coby Webb, another Fleetway pilot startles me. "Think she'll get us to Paris? In time to get back by Christmas? It'll be my first time back home for Christmas in Oklahoma in many a year."

I turn around to find Coby standing behind me in the freezing rain, smiling. "Sure, she'll get us to Paris in plenty of time. There's nothing better than being home for Christmas. Especially when home is Oklahoma. It's my home state too."

"How about that!" he says with a grin.

Looking back to the B-17, I confide to Coby, "I never thought I'd ever be flying the famous Flying Fortress."

We stand in silence looking at the lonely bomber in the dark freezing rain for a long while. When Coby turns to leave, I ask him, "Do you know where her flight manual is? I'd like to study it tonight."

He doesn't answer, so I try again. "What time are you checking me out in her tomorrow?"

Coby ignores my questions, pulls the collar up on his overcoat. His smile disappears, as he says, "We better get going. Narssarssuaq is eleven hours away, and only open during daylight hours. This time of year, in the Arctic, that means around ten in the morning until two in the afternoon. You ready?"

    I'm shocked. And for once I answer fast.

    "No. I'm not ready! This is the first B-17 I've ever even seen up close. I've never flown any four-engine planes before, no bombers at all."

    After my first T-6 delivery to Peru that scared me so badly, I decided I had worn out enough guardian angels for several lifetimes. I don't want to rush through any more check-outs in different airplanes, especially my first four-engine bomber. For emphasis I add, "The single-engine T-6 is a big airplane to me. I need to study the B-17 flight manual, and make some circuits around the field in her to learn how to fly this big bomber."

    Coby doesn't seem to be listening.

    "Come on, fellow Okie. Don't you want to be home for Christmas too?

    Being a kind man, he offers. "You can fly the first leg, I'll check you out en route."

    Then he grins, and says, "Just pretend like you're flying four T-6s, all at once. You'll do fine."

    He doesn't wait for an answer. As he starts off across the ramp, he hollers back. "Make sure all the tanks are full. I'm off to Operations to thaw out, check the weather, and file our flight plan."

Ferry pilots are always in a hurry. Maybe it's because they get paid only when they're flying. Or maybe they're dreaming of an extra hour's sleep, or a sit-down meal.

All I know is that I'm NOT ready to fly a four-engine bomber ... across the North Atlantic ... in freezing winter weather ... to Paris, France.

Left standing alone in the dark, under the famous bomber's huge wing, I contemplate what to do. Am I going to lose my dream job just because I'm scared? Rationalization begins again, as the freezing rain becomes large flakes of wet snow.

I wouldn't be here right now and have this opportunity to fly a B-17 if I hadn't made that first T-6 take-off in Miami, when I was so scared that my legs were shaking. Reading instruction manuals until I'm blue in the face won't actually teach me how to fly this beautiful bomber. The only way I learn is by doing. Sometimes we have to jump in with both feet and just do it. Even when we're scared.

We can't always have life the way we want it. If we always have to wait until we're ready, we'll miss out on a lot. Better to seize the opportunity. Go for the adventure. Have faith.

My little pep talk prepares me for the lights of the fuel truck arriving in the snowy darkness. I walk the 103 feet from wingtip to wingtip, looking for the fuel sump drains. The smiling crew chief driving the fuel truck motions me over to the belly of the bomber and shines his flashlight up on the large fuel tanks installed in her bomb bays. He grins, "She's got long legs. Thirteen hours to dry tanks."

She's a B-17G with her bomb bays converted to fuel tanks. She's being given to the Government of France under the Lend-Lease Program in support of their struggle in Vietnam. Her four enormous Wright 1820-97 engines develop 1,200 horsepower each, another gigantic leap for me. From one to four engines! From 650 to 4,800 horsepower!

By the time Coby comes back from Operations I've made sure that all her tanks are full, and have stowed my gear on board. Seated in the left seat of the cold cockpit, I'm studying the rows upon rows of instruments, dials, levers, radios, that are above, beside, in front of, and all around me. He crawls into the right seat and grunts. "Flight plan's on file. Time's a wastin'. Start 'em up."

He finds the check list in a side pocket, and begins reading. "Number one, fuel selector on main, boost pump on, prime, magnetos, start, mixture, check hydraulic pressure, cowl flaps open. Repeat for two, three, four."

With Coby pointing in the general direction, I find the necessary controls, valves, and switches to get number one and four started. Then engines two and three roar to life. With a salute to the crew chief standing in the blowing snow holding a large fire extinguisher, cold, and happy to see us leave, I start to taxi the big bomber. Straight for an icy ditch lit by red caution lights on the edge of the slick ramp.

With number one and two throttles open, three and four idling, the big bomber still won't turn for me. Coby gives it a try from the right seat before we run off the ramp. Same thing. She'll only go forward, heading straight for the drainage ditch.

Checking around the cockpit, Coby notices that her tail wheel lock is on, something I'd never heard of before. With a sheepish grin, he unlocks her tail wheel, and says, "She'll turn for you now." I open number one and two throttles again and she makes an immediate right turn, barely missing the drainage ditch as her big tires crunch through the snow and ice on the edge of the ramp.

After engine run-ups and pre-flight checks, it's now close to midnight as we sit at the end of the very long runway, waiting for our instrument clearance. I'm having serious second thoughts as I stare into the snowy blackness, punctuated by two rows of high intensity lights outlining the runway.

The blowing snow has restricted the visibility to less than half the length of the runway. Coby is talking. "It's a good thing they give Fleetway Captains their own clearance authority. Air Force Operations would never approve take-off in these conditions."

His comment only adds to my apprehension. I feel overwhelmed sitting there in the cockpit of my first four-engine bomber. Her instrument panel is lit up like a Christmas tree, with little red and green instrument lights glowing everywhere. Four of everything, four throttles, four propeller controls, four mixture controls, four fuel selector valves, four engine instrument clusters, four feather buttons.

Watching large flakes of wet snow blowing across the runway in the beam of our landing lights, I wonder if I'm out of my mind. A pilot who's been flying single-engine fighters about to take off in a four-engine bomber ... in the middle of the night ... into blowing snow ... low ragged ceiling ... poor visibility ... heavy icing conditions.

In an airplane with 4,800 horsepower ... that I just met late in the day .... to fly to a place eleven hours away ... half-way across the frigid North Atlantic ... to a place that I've never heard of, and can't pronounce anyway. Just because a fellow Okie is saying, "Come on, let's go. The tower's cleared us for take-off. Let's get out of here before they change their minds."

It's too late now to back out. My first four-engine take-off is beginning, ready or not, into night, instrument, icing conditions.

Coby continues. "Get those throttles up. I'll monitor the engine gauges, and call out speeds. All four fuel boosts are on. Get her rolling."

With a prayer in my heart, I slowly push her throttles up. My hand's not big enough to reach around all four throttles, so Coby flips on a bar below them to help to keep them even. With her tail wheel lock back on now, she keeps a steady course down the center line. She feels good.

Our weight is heavy, with her bomb bays full of 16,000 pounds of fuel to feed her four big engines for more than twelve hours. In spite of all that weight, she accelerates fast, lifting her tail to let me know she wants to fly.

There's the power of 4,800 horses pulling us through the snowy blackness, and she's ready to fly before I am. Coby's calling out the numbers, right beside me.

"V-1, engines looking good.

"V-2, establish climb, 120, 130 knots.

"Gear up, 140 knots.

"Flaps coming up.

"Better turn those landing lights off before they blind us."

As soon as we're airborne we're engulfed by the low clouds producing the big flakes of snow. The clouds are reflecting our landing lights, creating a glare but I don't know where the switches are located to turn them off.

Besides, I believe a pilot's first and foremost responsibility is to fly the airplane, and I'm not about to take my eyes off the instruments. Barely off the ground, and suspended in icy clouds, it takes every ounce of my concentration to keep the bomber climbing on a steady course, on instruments, in the turbulence.

"Sorry, but I don't know where the landing light switches are located. Would you please switch them off for me? I'm a little busy here."

Coby replies with a laugh. "Welcome to the world of four-engine airplanes, it does get a little busy at times. Sure, I'll get the lights off for you, the switches are right above your head."

Coby continues with the after take-off check list.

"Initial climb power.
"Flaps full up.
"Cowl flaps trailing.
"140, 150 airspeed.
"Left turn to zero-four-zero.
"Everything looking good."

We bounce along in the freezing clouds, leveling off at 9,000 feet, still embedded in the frozen precipitation. Out of the blackness suddenly a bright light is shining along the leading edge of our left wing. "What's that light out there?" I ask with a jump.

Coby laughs again, "Didn't mean to startle you. That's our de-ice lamp. I'm just checking for ice build-up on the wings. You'd better cycle the de-ice boots, it's starting to stick out there."

In the freezing cold with heavy snow, the de-ice boots have to be cycled about every twenty minutes to keep the ice from freezing on the wings. The boots are rubber coatings along the leading edge of the wings and tail surfaces which move just enough to break up the ice sticking to them. If they're left on constantly in heavy icing conditions, the ice can build up right over them, defeating their purpose, and destroying the lift of the wing.

With our air traffic control clearance in hand, and not much other traffic around in the wee hours of this cold winter night, the radio is fairly quiet. So Coby casually announces he's going back to get some sleep.

He must have noticed the startled look in my eyes. I'm only beginning to believe that MAYBE I can fly this big bomber with Coby right beside me to teach me. Now my "security blanket" announces he's going to sleep. Being considerate, he calls back as he disappears over the bomb bays, "If you have a problem, just call me."

He never even hears me answer, "How?"

The company I work for, Fleetway International, doesn't believe in co-pilots, navigators, flight engineers, or radio operators. Only captains, who are expected to be competent to fly all types of aircraft, and perform the other duties as well. If a plane to be ferried is transport category, four-engine, or otherwise requires two pilots, two captains are dispatched, who fly alternate legs.

Hour after hour we droned into the icy blackness. After the cramped cockpits of the fighters, I'm enchanted by the roomy bomber cockpit with all the colored lights.

Still engulfed in snow-laden clouds, there's nothing to see outside, so I turn the cockpit lights up and begin studying the check lists, memorizing where the important controls are located. Every twenty minutes I check for wing ice and recycle the boots. By the time the sun comes up, the cockpit is as familiar to me as the living room of my parents home in Oklahoma, only colder.

The clouds are beginning to thin as it's now too cold to snow. An angry and cold North Atlantic Ocean is becoming visible through the gaps in the clouds below, full of whitecaps and icebergs. It's so cold in the cockpit that I have to scrape the ice off the inside of the windows to see out. I don't know how to start the gasoline heater, and I'm afraid of igniting the fumes and blowing us up if I try.

Outside air temperature started out in the 20s, but has steadily fallen into the minus numbers now. The extreme cold is what finally woke up Coby as we approached the massive iceshelf of Greenland. He's a little blue, and a lot grumpy.

"What are you, some kind of Eskimo? Thought you said you were an Okie. It never gets this cold in Oklahoma. Why are we flying without heat in this arctic weather?"

I look up at him and reply honestly. "I don't know how to fire up the heater."

With patience born of teaching many, Coby shows me how to prime the heater with avgas, and ignite it with a roar, but no vapors. My, it does make a difference. Instead of frosted glass, our cockpit becomes like a cozy little heated room with a picture window showing the pretty landscape up ahead. The ice cap of Greenland is just visible on the horizon, and the ocean is now full of giant icebergs, brilliant white with just a hint of blue, reflecting the cold water.

I'm admiring the view when Coby reminds me it's time to report in to Narssassaquak Control. He has to repeat it several times for me to learn how to say Nar-ssas-sa-quak.

"Narssassaquak Control, seven-niner-two.
"Estimating Blondie four-four, twelve thousand feet."

The radio crackles to life.

"Roger seven-niner-two, Narssassaquak.
"Descend to four thousand feet.
"Altimeter one-zero-one-three millibars.
"Report Blondie."

As we descend, the ice bergs become like islands, and the ice cap of Greenland appears as a wall of solid ice looming ahead. Coby tells me about Greenland's ice cap.

"With an average elevation of 8,000 feet, the ice cap is mostly pure ice deposited during eons of violent storms descending from the North Pole. The ice never has a chance to melt in the always freezing temperatures so it just keeps piling up. The southern tip of Greenland is surrounded by huge hunks of her ice shelf which have broken off, making an impenetrable barrier of icebergs to all except those who fly."

Over the ice covered coast now, at a remotely operated radio beacon, I report in.

"Narssassaquak Control, seven-niner-two.

"Over Blondie four-two.

"Estimating Dagwood zero-one.

"Four thousand feet."

The Air Force tower responds quickly.

"Roger seven-niner-two, Narssassaquak.

"Weather, high cirrus, wind zero-eight-zero degrees, twelve knots, temperature minus two-two.

"Cleared to enter fjord, descend to 1500 feet.

"Report sunken ship."

Coby fills me in on the details. "Narssassaquak is a small U.S. Air Force base built during World War II for the refueling of military planes en route to and from the European theater. Sitting at the end of a small winding fjord, it was well protected from German submarines, but there is no room for an instrument approach. A missed approach puts you into the 8,000 foot high wall of ice rising perpendicular from the end of the runway to the ice cap of Greenland.

"Since the weather is usually icy and dicey around here, the Air Force installed two low-frequency beacons. Bluie West One, affectionally called Blondie by the military pilots, on the coast to use for making a let-down over the ocean. Blondie also identifies the fjord leading to Narssassaquak from dozens of others looking exactly the same.

"Bluie West Two, nicknamed Dagwood, is located at the end of the one-way runway at Narssassaquak Air Force Base. But you can't fly direct between the two radio beacons because of the icy mountains in between. After letting down over the ocean you have to visually snake your way up the fjord, low and slow. Turning with every bend, trying to avoid the other fjords that will lead you into blind canyons of ice with no room to turn around. Many aircraft that didn't make it, lie at the bottom of the fjords, or covered by snow and ice among the icy mountains.

"A supply ship that made a wrong turn and sank in the icy fjord is the only landmark to keep you from doing the same between Blondie and Dagwood. You must always find the sunken ship. If you don't see it, better high-tail it back out to Blondie while you still can, because you're in the wrong fjord. When you find the sunken ship, remember to turn LEFT, or you'll end up in the same frozen grave."

We're down to 1,500 feet, looking for all we're worth for the sunken ship. I'm following the meandering fjord, twisting and turning with every bend, trying to keep the big bomber in the main branch of the frozen fjord between solid ice walls up to 8,000 feet.

After more than eleven hours flying, our bomber is thirsty, and like a tired eagle looking for home.

CHAPTER 7

B-17 To Paris   Part II
Year 1953   Age 22

*"Security is a myth. Life is full of risks.
Without God watching over us,
we'd never survive."*

We never saw it coming. And we were both looking straight out the windshields, scanning for the sunken ship.

In an instant, a fraction of a second, both windshields are covered by the dirty underbelly of a jet fighter in a steep bank.

There is no time to take any evasive action … to dive … to turn … or even to think. How the jet is able to miss us, by inches, as it passes overhead I will never know. It came at us head-on out of nowhere, and is gone in an instant.

The shock of an almost certain, fatal, mid-air collision steals my voice, and all Coby can utter is a loud moan.

Another jet fighter is dead ahead ... screaming towards us. The pilot's helmeted head is visible for a split second as he frantically dives to miss us.

Another jet ... and another ... and another ... keeps filling our windshields.

A beehive of jet fighters, all trying desperately to miss us. One's in a vertical bank to the right ... another's banking left. Others are diving or climbing to pass over, or under us. There's no way to get out of their way, or anywhere to go in the narrow fjord.

They're all around us, in very unusual attitudes. The jets are almost out of control, doing everything they can to avoid hitting us.

Coby's voice is gone now too. We just sit there, sure the next one will hit us dead on, and it will all be over with, forever. At least it will be fast.

When close to death I've heard that sometimes your whole life flashes back very rapidly. This is certainly the closest I have ever been to dying, but my life seems to go forward, and slows down into very slow, slow motion. Like those old movies when the film is about to break.

V e r y ... v e r y ... s l o w l y.   One ... little ... step ... at ... a ... time.   I ... can ... now ...see ... the ... jet ... fighters ... coming ... at ... us ... very ... very ... slowly.   Banking ... steeply ... diving.   The ... frantic ... look ... in ... the ...

pilot's ... eyes ... when ... he ... realizes ... he's ... going ... to ... hit ... us ... dead-on.

A blinding flash ... a fireball of exploding fuel ... the ... slow ... falling ... of ... small ...pieces ... of ... shiny ... metal ... from ... a ... new ... jet ... fighter, ... and ... an ... old ... bomber, ... into ... the ... icy ... fjord.

I can see my mother standing at the front door of our family home in Ponca City, Oklahoma, being handed a telegram. Mother and Dad sitting on the divan in the living room, reading the telegram over and over again, crying.

My sister, Carolyn, on the telephone, tears streaming down her face, saying, "No, it can't be Jerrie, she's such a careful pilot. There must be some mistake."

No, no, no. That's what hurts the most. Not dying, but hurting those who love me. That's when I realize that our lives do not belong to us alone, to do with as we please. A part of us will always belong to those who love us, and they are deeply affected by our actions. Those who gave us the gift of life, nurtured us, taught us. And loved us enough to give us the freedom to find our own way. God, our parents, family, friends.

As quickly as it began, it's all over. How we are still flying, Coby and I do not understand. But we are, and it's quiet all around. The steady drone of the B-17's powerful engines doesn't enter my consciousness, just the silence, as I say, "Thank you, God."

Beads of sweat run down our foreheads as Coby and I look around to assess the damage, then at each other. Our B-17 isn't even scratched! We know a miracle when we see one, and we have just lived through one.

We aren't even upset with the Air Force air traffic controller. He just about cost us our lives by clearing a squadron of F-86 "Shooting Star" jet fighters for take-off from Narssassaquak, and down the one-way fjord, after clearing us inbound. We're just grateful to be alive. My guardian angel is working overtime.

Shaken, we continue up the fjord, find the sunken ship, turn left. Before long I spy the runway at the end of the fjord, and report on long final to Narssassaquak Air Force Base.

The Tower comes right back.

"Roger seven-niner-two, Narssassaquak Control.

"We have you in sight, cleared to land.

"Wind zero-seven-zero degrees, ten knots.

"Check gear down and locked."

Then he adds, "Sorry about the traffic in the fjord."

Coby's reading the check list.

"Gear down, three green, tail wheel lock on.

"Approach speed 120 knots.

"Props forward, high rpm.

"Full flaps, slow her down.

"Hold her off, o f f."

She's light as a feather after feeding her four thirsty engines for eleven hours, twenty-six minutes, and wants to float down the runway, even in the freezing temperature. She reminds me of my old circus Cub that used to float while landing in pastures, on hot summer afternoons in the Great Plains.

When the bomber finally gives up flying she settles down on all three points, ever so gently, a real lady. She never strays from the center line, even on the ice-covered runway. My fear of flying a big, powerful four-engine bomber just evaporates into her icy tracks as we taxi behind the "follow me" Jeep to the refueling ramp.

Coby and I feel pretty washed-out after the almost mid-air collision. We want nothing more than to button her down, and head for the Bachelors Officers Quarters to unwind and catch up on some sleep. But that's a luxury ferry pilots seldom have.

There's only two hours of daylight left to get refueled, cleared outbound, and back down the fjord. The wind is coming up, and if we don't get out soon, we could be stuck here for endless days in the next polar blast to this place, well known for blizzards, ice worms, and St. Elmo's fire.

Once again Coby does the flight planning, while I supervise refueling. The high octane fuel is stored in above ground tanks, and it takes a long time to pump almost 18,000 pounds of avgas into her large bomb bay tanks.

The cold temperature is beginning to get to me as the wind picks up. Snow begins falling again as we taxi back out the ice-covered runway, at 1:30 in the afternoon, less than an hour before dark.

It's Coby's leg to fly, while I call off the check lists. We have to get down the fjord before it socks in, find the sunken ship, and get out to Blondie visually, before nightfall.

Halfway down the fjord, while still looking for the sunken ship, we hear on the radio from Narssassaquak Control.

"Notice to all aircraft in the area.

"Narssassaquak Air Force Base is officially closed to all air traffic.

"Weather, one-quarter mile visibility, blowing snow.

"Ceiling two hundred feet, obscured.

"Wind zero-two-zero degrees, gusting to fifty-five knots.

"Bluie West Two beacon off."

The weather continues to deteriorate, but we find the sunken ship and turn right. After passing Blondie, we begin climbing through the snow-laden clouds. Turning back east, we come across Blondie again at 8,000 feet. And continue climbing to 12,000 feet, to top Greenland's ice cap with easy grace.

It's a little after two in the afternoon, and pitch black again, as we bounce along in the turbulent, icy clouds. For once, I'm glad I'm not flying, and I crawl across the bomb bay to find Coby's sleeping bag and try to get warm. After lying there shaking for about half an hour, I finally warm up enough to settle in for a long winter's nap, secure in the knowledge that we're in good hands.

But my mind won't let my body sleep. There is so much to think about. About what happened in the fjord. About how we almost died through no fault of our own. About how we're still alive through no action of our own. About God. About what's important in life. About the things I would miss so much. The love of family, friends. The song of a bird, the flight of a butterfly, the smell of honeysuckle.

After a couple of hours mulling it all over I decide that no matter how careful we are, it's never enough. Security is a myth. Life is full of risks. Without God watching over us, we'd never survive. After getting warm in the sleeping bag, I crawl back across the bomb bay to the cockpit.

Coby comments. "Well, that wasn't much of a sleep. What's the matter? Still thinking about our almost mid-air? Me, too."

Wanting to change the subject, I wonder aloud. "Why are the daylight hours so short up here on the North Atlantic? We've been gone over sixteen hours, and have only had a few hours of daylight, back there in Greenland. Now it's dark again, in the middle of the afternoon."

"Remember your solar tables, Jerrie. It's December, and we're pretty far north. Some places in the arctic don't get any daylight at all this time of year. Don't come back in the summer though, if you're a light sleeper. It's just the opposite then, daylight all the time, only a few hours of darkness around midnight in this area.

"We're coming up on the winter solstice. Shortest day of the year. We'll be in Paris so we can sleep through the longest night. Pretty good planning, huh?"

Leave it to a ferry pilot to think of that. If there's anything ferry pilots like to do more than fly, it's sleep. I tease, "Why Coby, I thought you'd take me out on the town, and show me Paris when we get in."

He replies without hesitation. "Lady, you're on your own in Paris. I'm heading straight for a nice soft, warm, bed. And after a good long sleep, I'm hopping an airline to New York, then Oklahoma for Christmas with my family. I have even more to be grateful for now."

After almost thirteen hours flying through snow and ice again, we break out over Paris in the dark freezing rain. We hear on the radio that LeBourget Airport is open, so we cancel our instrument flight plan, and look for a break in the clouds that will allow a visual approach. We have enough fuel reserve to go on to our alternate, Rome, but not enough to wait out the long "stack" of airliners holding over Paris waiting for instrument landing clearances.

We're flying in the clear between the high clouds producing light freezing rain, and thin broken stratus below, with the lights of Paris shining through. I see some clearing up ahead.

"There's a break up there, maybe we can get down there."

Coby guides our Flying Fortress towards the lights. "Quick, gear down, twenty degree flaps. We can let down here visually."

What a gorgeous sight! The whole spread-out city of Paris, with billions of lights glowing from horizon to horizon. The freezing rain makes each little light glisten. But there's no time to enjoy the pretty sights, we've still got to find LeBourget airport.

"It's got to be right up there," Coby says, pointing with his nose. "Keep an eye out for antennas, and the Eiffel Tower. They're higher than we are right now. See anything on your side?" he asks anxiously.

"Yes, some dark areas. Looks like hills, Are there hills in Paris? Wait a sec. Coby, some lights just went by our wingtip. ABOVE our right wing!"

Coby's reaction is immediate. He starts a maximum climb. "That's it! Gear up, max power. We're going back up. Get on the radio and ask for a clearance to Rome."

Reaching for the gear handle, out of the corner of my eye I catch the swing of a white rotating beacon of an airport dead ahead.

"Wait, there it is, at least some airport. See, there's the runway lights at two o'clock."

A big grin spreads across Coby's face. "Oh, you're soooo right What a nice sight! Leave the gear down. We're going in.

"LeBourget Tower, seven-niner-two.

"Seven miles south, visual, for landing."

With only a slight French accent, the tower replies in English.

"Roger seven-niner-two, LeBourget Tower.

"Cleared straight in, runway three-five.

"Wind three-three-zero degrees, twelve knots."

A few minutes later.

"Seven-niner-two, LeBourget, we have you in sight, cleared to land."

Squeal, squeal, the main gear tires sound, as Coby makes a perfect wheel landing on the slick LeBourget runway. Taxiing in, he turns to me and says, "Welcome to Paris. By the grace of God we're here. I'm gonna go find that bed I've been promising myself."

After sleeping through the longest night of the year, we turn our big bomber over to the French Air Force the next day. They will outfit her with new radios, radar, and other equipment, before flying her on to Vietnam. There she will be used to supply the French forces isolated in Dien Bien Phu, surrounded by the enemy.

About all I get to see of Paris is her twinkly lights shining through freezing rain. After less than twenty-four hours in the "City of Lights" we catch Air France back to New York at night, or maybe it's daytime. It's hard to tell, since I'm not wearing a watch, and we're still in the land of winter darkness. The freezing rain is still coming down.

Today is the shortest day of the year. The others just seemed like it.

During the nine-hour flight on Air France, Coby and I talk about how special Christmas is. How we are alive right now, literally, by the grace of God. How great it will be to share Christmas with our families in Oklahoma this year. We can hardly wait to step off the Air France plane and onto another airliner headed to Oklahoma.

In New York we check in with Fleetway Operations, where we are handed new orders from the main base at Lockheed Air Terminal in Burbank, California.

"Captains Webb and Cobb are to proceed immediately to Teterboro Airport, pick up Douglas DC-3 Serial No. 3724 and deliver to United States Air Force Air Depot, Miami."

Coby and I just look at each other.

Tired, sleepy, unshaven, Coby expresses his entire sentiment in two words, "I quit."

I start thinking fast. "It's late, but if we head straight for Teterboro, and the DC-3 is ready, we can leave by midnight. Fly all night again, deliver the "three" to the Air Force in Miami tomorrow, catch an airliner out of Miami tomorrow night, and still make it home to Oklahoma on Christmas Eve.

"How about it Coby? You can curl up in your sleeping bag in the back of the "three" and sleep the whole time. I'll fly us to Miami. The East Coast is like my old 'stomping grounds' after all those T-6 deliveries."

Coby just keeps shaking his head, side to side.

After flying a B-17 across the North Atlantic, a DC-3 to Miami sounds to me like a good way to get warm again, so I keep trying to convince him.

"C'mon Coby, let's go to Teterboro, pick up the 'three', and fly it to Miami. We'll still make it home to Oklahoma for Christmas. And you won't have to quit."

Now it's me that's in a hurry. Guess I'm catching the ferry pilot's occupational disease.

Coby isn't thrilled with the idea, but he finally agrees to it. Missing a few more nights (and days) of sleep, we ferry the DC-3 to the Air Force in Miami. And we still get to Oklahoma late on Christmas Eve, with much to celebrate ... the gift of life itself, anew.

BOOK III

Jack, World's Altitude Record, Astronaut?

8. Jack ... Part I
     Year 1953   Age 22   page 105
       Over water emergency
       Stretching for Jamaica
       Deadstick landing

9. Jack ... Part II
     Years 1953-1955   Age 22-24   page 115
       Cleaning up
       Jamaica
       Private cove

10. Aero Commander to World's Altitude Record
     Year 1959   Age 28   page 131
       Climbing, ice
       Almost stalling
       Another World Record

11. Flight To Space?
     Years 1959-1963   Age 28-32   page 143
       Announcement, Press
       NASA Consultant
       Congressional hearing

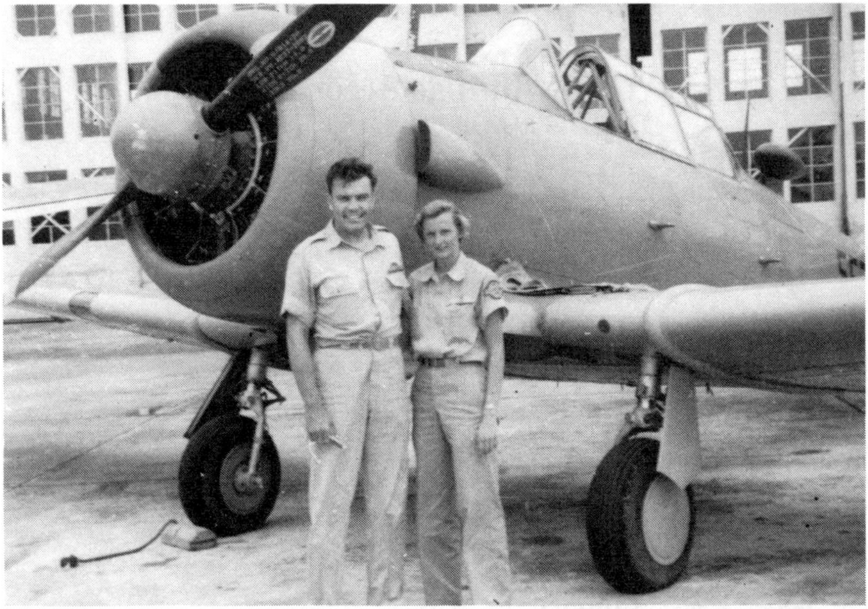

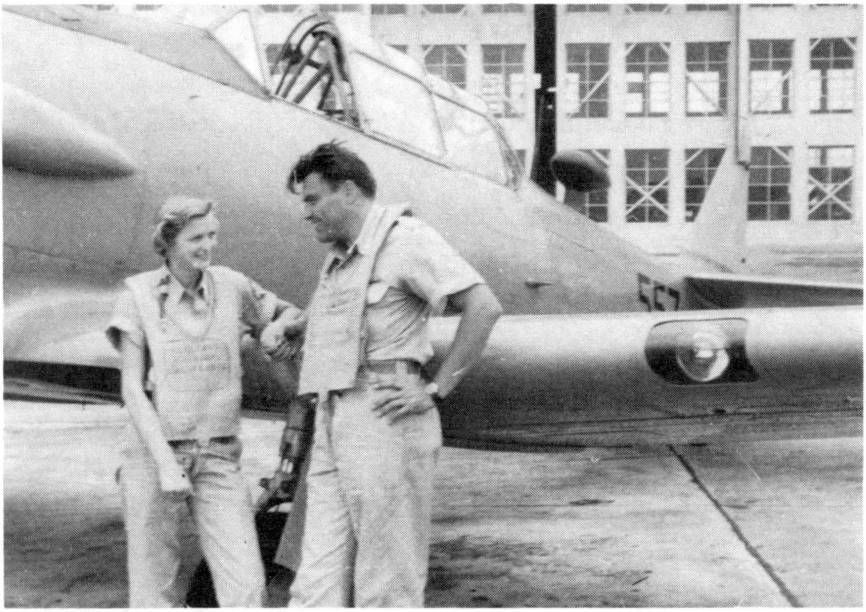

CHAPTER 8

Jack Part I
Year 1953 Age 22

"Ditch a T-6 in mid-ocean?
Nothing to it, piece of cake.
The love of my life is with me."

It isn't part of my plans. Not at this time in my life. I'm much too busy in my dream job, as an international ferry pilot. It's my dream come true, and I wouldn't give it up for anything.

Flying is more important to me. I love spending the many hours in the air, seeing the beauty of the sky, oceans, islands, continents.

There'll be time for that later. I've only begun my life's adventure, and I've a lot more to see, learn, and do, as a solo pilot.

Falling in love is not in my flight plan for now. Of course I've thought about it a lot, but flying is my life, and who would put up with that?

Wham! Before I even know what is happening, here I am, head over heels in love. With another pilot yet! And, worst of all, with my boss!

Jack, his charm, rugged good looks, and charisma certainly hadn't gone unnoticed by me. Without a doubt he was the best pilot I've ever known, and certainly the most handsome.

Some of the Fleetway pilots talked about the movie starlets Jack dated when he was back tending to business in Fleetway's main office at Lockheed Air Terminal in Burbank, California. Certainly no hope for a "plain Jane" like me. And besides, I'm totally happy ferrying airplanes all over the world, and content to admire him from a distance.

On the rare occasion when Jack ferried a T-6 to Peru with me, I was thrilled. There was so much I learned from him. About flying, of course, but he's also taught me mundane things like how to tie my uniform tie. How to give a proper salute. How to drain fuel sumps without getting avgas down my armpit. And I finally caught onto the hang of formation flying under his tutelage.

Now he's back, after seven months, ferrying another T-6 to Lima with me. Each time we're together I enjoy him more. His marvelous sense of humor, his honesty, and, ... when my T-6 lost a propeller seal over the ocean, he was right there for me.

Flying over the Caribbean, between Cuba and Jamaica, in beautiful weather, we were visiting over the radio. "Flying that B-17 was sure fun, even in all the snow and ice and ..." Suddenly there's a loud "pop," and oil starts streaming from my engine.

"Jack, my prop seal's blown. Oil's all over the canopy. Can't see outside, I'm flying by instruments now."

Jack's reaction is immediate. "I'm off your left wing, coming in closer now. Keep her straight and level. Fly one-five-eight degrees. Pull your prop control all the way back. Call out your engine oil pressure."

"As soon as the seal blew, I pulled the prop control back. But oil pressure's still dropping, down to 24 psi now."

"Wish I could trade planes with you. Looks like we'll have to ditch. We're too far out to return to Cuba, and Jamaica's another eighty miles. I doubt we can make it. Keep calling out your oil pressure."

"Down to 18 psi now. What do you mean WE'LL have to ditch?"

"Pull your raft out from under your parachute and attach the lanyard. Check your Mae West straps. Stow your charts, flight log, clearances. Get everything ready to ditch. No loose items in the cockpit that can turn into projectiles in a crash.

"You'll need help landing in those waves blind. I'm going in with you. Call out pressure."

I'm shocked. "Jack, you wouldn't lose a good airplane just because I have to? I'll be fine. Pressure is 14 psi, ah, 12 now."

"How will you calculate surface winds, altitude, wave patterns, attitude, with no forward visibility? Pay attention, you're off your heading. Turn to one-five-two degrees now. Call out oil pressure."

"The oil's seeping into the cockpit now, everything's covered, including my instruments. Wait, I have to find something to wipe it off with. Ah ... ah ... it looks like a little below 10 psi"

"Hold as much altitude as you can, but get ready to ditch. Call out procedures."

"Raft ready, lanyard attached. Mae West straps secure. Charts, loose items stored. Canopy cracked. Oops, oil's really pouring in now with the canopy ajar. Everything's covered, including me. Gotta wipe off the gauge again. Yeah, it's still dropping, looks like around 7 psi now.

"I'll need your help with headings, speeds, attitude as all the instruments are covered with oil. But please Jack, don't go in with me. I know about rafts, and I'm a strong swimmer. I'll make it through."

"Forget about the oil. Forget what the book says, slide your canopy all the way back and jam it with something. Or it'll slam shut on impact, and you'll drown because you won't be able to get out. I'm with you all the way, airplanes are expendable, good pilots are not."

He hesitates, then adds, "I didn't wait thirty-six years to lose the love of my life now."

I can hardly believe what I've just heard. Did he really say "love of my life?" Can he truly feel the same as I do?

I feel a happy grin start across my face. Oil drips off my chin. Nothing else matters. Ditch a T-6 in mid-ocean? Nothing to it, piece of cake. The love of my life is with me.

"You still there? Call out oil pressure."

"Huh, oh, yes, gotta wipe off the gauge. Ah, ah, it's bouncing off zero, as best as I can see. Maybe 3 psi, at the most."

"We're going to try for a long glide to the Jamaican coast. I can just see it now on the horizon, about thirty miles dead ahead."

Grinning ear to ear, I reply, "Whatever you say, love of my life."

Now the silence is on Jack's end. Until things get busy. There's a lilt to Jack's voice when he says, "Hallelujah, we've got it made!

"Shut her down, love. Maybe we can save the engine as well as your plane. Not only is the Jamaican coast within gliding range, but there's a nice long runway running right alongside. Montego Bay International Airport is right down there, just waiting for you."

Jack reports in to Air Traffic Control.

"Kingston Control, FAP five-eight-eight.

"Please cancel our flight plan, two-plane formation, Miami to Kingston. We're landing Montego Bay."

Then he calls Montego Control Tower.

"Montego Tower, FAP five-eight-eight. Two-plane formation, one without power, five miles north. Request immediate landing."

The Montego Tower responds instantly.

"Roger, FAP five-eight-eight, we're looking ... ah ... ah ... in sight. Cleared to land, any runway."

"Wind zero-six-zero degrees, eight knots."

"Altimeter one-zero-one-eight millibars."

"Emergency vehicles alerted."

Jack's smiling voice continues on the intercom.

"O.K., my love, start turning now, to one-niner-zero degrees. Your speed is 140 knots, four miles out."

"I know you can't read your gauges, just turn a little more to the right, and hold her speed where she feels comfortable. I'm still on your left wing, and I'll call out speeds and headings. We need to stay close in, you've only got one chance this time, without power.

"Start left turn now, not too steep, keep coming around ... until ... until ... now.

"Straighten out, nice and easy, trim up, start flaps down.

"Hold her steady, you're now at 120 knots.

"Gear down, locked.

"Left just a bit, oops, too much. Back right just a hair.

"Straight now, flaps full down. Check gear down, lock on. 90 knots.

"Level off, you're over the runway now.

"Slow her down some more, straight ahead, looking good.

"Nose up, hold her off ... o f f ... o f f."

Blinded by the oil, I hold the control stick back and wait in silence for the crash, or the ... there it is now ... the beautiful squeal, squeal of two tires touching a hot hard surface, complaining at having to go from standing still to sixty mph in a tiny fraction of a second.

Jack lands in formation off my left wing, still singing on the radio.

"Right rudder, just a touch.

"Easy on the brakes.

"A little bit to your left.

"Not too bad for a deadstick, in the blind. In fact one of your better landings, love. Congratulations."

Grateful to be safely down on land, and dry except for the oil all over me, I utter a heartfelt, "Thank you, God."

Then, to the matters at hand.

"Thanks, love. But how do I clear the runway, without power?"

"Sit tight, I'm on my way." Jack answers.

Within seconds I feel my plane shudder as Jack jumps up on the wing, slips in the oil, and crashes into my open canopy.

His strong arms are lifting me out of the cockpit, oil and all. Crash vehicles are speeding down the runway, sirens screaming. But all I hear is Jack saying, "I couldn't bear to lose you," as he holds me close, on the oil-covered wing of my crippled airplane.

After we slide off the slick wing together, he swings me around in circles, feet off the ground, right in the middle of the runway. I feel giddy, light-headed, filled with a happiness I haven't known before.

Tears don't mix too well with oil. Jack tries to wipe mine away, making it worse. I try to wipe the streaks from his face with my oily hands, smearing them more. We give up, laugh at the sight of each other covered with used engine oil, and embrace again.

The crash wagons screech to a stop surrounding our airplanes on the runway. The well-trained crash crews come running towards us, dragging their heavy hoses and crash axes.

They're a little surprised to find their "casualties" laughing, hugging, dancing in circles in their oil-covered khakis. They stop in midstream, disappointed there are no "survivors" to rescue, or airplane crash fire to fight. But smiles brighten their faces as they watch two people in love celebrating life in the middle of the runway.

The ambulance attendants want to rush us off to the hospital to be checked over. We decline their kind offer, preferring to ride in the back of the tow truck as it tows my oil-covered T-6 to the hangar, and returns for Jack's airplane.

Slowly, reality returns as Jack's booming voice on the hangar telephone is saying, "Tell them to get someone down here on the double who knows how to install propeller seals right the first time. And have every prop seal replaced on the remaining planes in Trenton. We almost lost our best T-6 pilot because of their dumb mistake.

"One more thing. I'm unreachable the next few days."

Jack hangs up the old-fashioned telephone earpiece, walks over to where I'm sitting on the hangar floor, sort of in a daze.

"Are you alright, Hon? After we get this oil off of us we're going to go stretch out on a beach. O.K.?"

I just smile, words seem superfluous.

Jack drains the fuel sump of my plane into a pile of newspapers he's gathered on the Quonset hut hangar floor. Sitting on the floor beside my T-6, we begin blotting the oil off each other. We soak up most of it with the papers, but now we're covered with oil smudges mixed with green dye from the avgas, and black newsprint ink.

He climbs up on the oily wing to retrieve my B-4 bag from the rear cockpit. Handing it down to me, and pointing to an open door, he says, "You'll feel better after a shower and a change to some clean clothes. Got some strong shampoo?"

I nod and disappear into the one "facility" in the old World War II hangar. Just as I'm closing the door I hear Jack talking to the tall Jamaican mechanic who has been standing there, just watching us. "I know it says m-e-n, but you guard that door with your life. If anyone comes within ten yards, you tackle them. There's a lady in there."

Shampoo and oil do not mix. After three tries, I give up. Now the shampoo, engine oil, gas dye, and newsprint ink is all stuck in what used to be limp blond hair, but now is a gooey green mess. So what? I'm alive. I'm in love.

Jack is still cleaning up the oily mess on the hangar floor when I exit the well-guarded men's room. He looks up, smiles.

"Hey, that does look better. I like your green hair. My turn now, out in a jiffy."

CHAPTER 9

Jack   Part II
Year 1953-55   Age 22-24

*"We found perfect happiness in
an imperfect world.
Our joy had no bounds."*

The world is his home, and his hobby is making friends. Jack rarely asks for anything for himself, but this time he does.

The tower chief is talking with the mechanic, waiting for Jack, when he comes out of the men's room.

"Hi, old buddy. You didn't have to arrive like THAT to get our attention."

Jack smiles broadly, greets his Jamaican friend, Isaiah, with a bear hug. He introduces me, asks about each of Isaiah's family by name, and continues. "I promised Jerrie I'd take her for that swim we didn't get out there with the sharks in mid-ocean. Know where I can get a car?"

Without missing a beat, Isaiah says.

"Sure, take mine, for as long as you want. It's sitting right over there in the tower lot. Not very fancy, but it'll get you where you're going. Help yourself, I'll catch rides with my friends."

As we start walking towards his car, Isaiah continues. "Here's a better idea. It's been pretty quiet in the tower lately, and I've got some leave time coming. Why don't you two just relax, and I'll drive you to the best beach on this island. None of that touristy stuff. I'll show you the Jamaica only we Jamaicans know. The good parts we save for ourselves."

It sounds good to Jack. "Can't pass up an offer like that. Let's go."

After Isaiah makes a few phone calls we leave on the most romantic interlude I ever imagined. Jack visits with Isaiah in the front seat, while I fuss with my gooey green hair in the back seat. First stop is a pharmacy where Isaiah buys a bottle of something he says might help dissolve the mess in my hair. I sprinkle it on and try to comb it through. It does help, and fills the car with the aroma of bay rum.

The next stop is a thatched hut on the beach where fresh fish is being cooked on an open grill. We discover we are famished as Isaiah keeps bringing us large banana leaves filled with broiled whole fish and breadfruit. We sit on driftwood in the sand, eating the fresh cooked fish with our fingers, picking the tender meat from the bones. And munching on the hot roasted breadfruit, washing it all down with icy Cokes. The joyful sounds of Jamaica and her people, the lilt of their voices as they sing their words as much as speak them, is like music to me.

After the late lunch we drive for hours along the north shore of Jamaica, enjoying the beautiful tropical scenery. Hibiscus blooming in every shade of the rainbow, tulip trees with their flaming blooms reaching skyward, ferns in dozens of shades of green.

Despite the large lunch, we can't resist the fresh fruits offered at roadside stands. Every now and then we stop at thatched huts by the roadside to enjoy the sweet pawpaws, tart kumquats, juicy mangos, cooked plantains.

At one roadside stand where we stop around dusk, about thirty people are sitting on the wooden steps of a small store, singing gospel songs. Isaiah brings us Cokes while Jack and I join the singers on the steps. Their rhythm is so contagious we can't resist for long before joining in, singing "I'll fly away, fly away, oh glory, I'll fly away, fly away. To a land on heaven's golden shore, oh I'll fly away, fly away."

Just after dark we take a left turn down a goat trail to a protected cove where the blue Caribbean shimmers in the moonlight. We can see the waves crashing on a reef across the mouth of the cove. After they regroup in the gentle breeze of the cove, the waves break gently again, massaging the rosy sand beach.

Isaiah drives his old car right onto the beach, parking next to a weathered wood platform. Jack and I run, holding hands, straight for the surf, diving into the biggest breaker we see, clothes and all.

Coming up for air, Jack pulls me towards him. He's trying to talk with a mouthful of sea water. "See, I told you we were going in the ocean together."

Without even thinking I say, "My love, that's when I knew we were kindred spirits, that we would always be together."

Right then and there, standing in the surf, in wet clothes and green hair, Jack gently pulls me closer, and kisses me. It's a good thing he's holding me, for I feel myself melting, floating happily out to sea, forever in his arms.

Isaiah has found some dry bamboo, and is building a bonfire on the beach. As we come sloshing up from the surf he shows us where he has buried a dozen or so coconuts in the sand to keep cool. Handing an opened one to each of us, he shows us how to drink the milk and dig out the coconut meat with a piece of the shell.

When he points out a small open-top three-sided enclosure among the palm trees, with a rain-water tank above, I happily rush off to wash my hair again, and don dry clothes.

Isaiah was raised in this part of Jamaica, Portland Parish, and walks up the hill behind the cove to visit his relatives. Jack heads for the open-air shower and a change to dry clothes, while I arrange sticks by the fire to dry our wet clothes. Then we sit on pieces of driftwood, watching the breakers roll in.

Jack is remembering the events of the morning.

"You know, you were pretty brave out there over the ocean."

"No, I've never been brave in my whole life. I've never been in love either."

Jack likes to kid. "Anyone I know? Who's the lucky man?"

"You're teasing, Jack. No one in the whole wide world could be happier than I am right now."

When Isaiah returns with jerked pork and chicken, wrapped in banana leaves with fragrant bay leaves, we discover our appetites are raging again. Roasting breadfruit on the bonfire, picking mangos from the trees, and with coconut milk to drink, we have a virtual banquet on our tropical beach.

Isaiah has borrowed three hammocks from his relatives, and ties them between the palm trees on the beach. We stay the night in this idyllic spot, watching the moon set over the Blue Mountains. I fall asleep listening to the breaking waves of the tide coming in, as Isaiah quiets the fire.

"Good morning, my love."

Jack is already up, shaved, holding a hollowed-out gourd full of what looks like scrambled eggs, but smells like fish.

"Isaiah's fixed Jamaica's national dish for our breakfast, dried fish cooked with the fruit of the ackee tree. If the ackees are picked too green, or too ripe, they're toxic, can kill you. But Isaiah picked these just right this morning. He guarantees it'll start our day off with a happy smile."

I devour it without a thought to it's toxicity. It occurs to me that if being in love gives me this kind of appetite, I may end up weighing 300 pounds.

We prefer to stay in our pretty cove, but Isaiah wants to show us where he played as a child in the caves among the hills behind the cove. Hiking on goat trails, playing hide-and-seek in the caves of Nonsuch, we have fun. But we hurry back to our secluded cove.

Even words are coming easier for me.

"I've never been so happy in my entire life, and I haven't even thought of flying, or airplanes, all day!" That thought comes as a complete surprise to me.

Jack smiles. "You mean there's something more important to you than flying?"

"You're teasing again, Jack. How can we be so fortunate to find each other in this whole vast universe? Some people spend a lifetime looking, and never find that one person meant just for them."

For the first time in my life, I almost enjoy talking. But listening is still better.

Jack muses. "You're only twenty-two. I had to wait longer than you, thirty-six years! Are you sure you'll love me as deeply when I'm an old man of seventy-six, and you're just a youngster of sixty-two?"

My words rush from my heart. "More so! Yesterday I thought I couldn't possibly love you more, but today it's true, I love you even more. Just imagine, how great it will be in forty years. How will we contain it all?"

Jack looks puzzled, then grins. "I don't know. But I'd sure like to try."

I rest my head on his chest, thinking of spending the rest of our lives together.

"Grow old along with me, the best is yet to be."

Suddenly I'm hungry again, and ask, "Any more coconuts?"

Jack picks up the last coconut hull, peers inside, shakes it. "Nope, we drank them all. Guess we'd better go find some more to bury."

Wandering hand in hand along the beach, we gather more coconuts than we can carry in just a short walk. While Jack cuts the tops off of two of them with Isaiah's machete, and buries the others in the sand, I pick mangos, humming along with the cicadas.

With coconuts free for the looking, and tropical trees loaded with fruits, I could stay here forever ... with my beloved ... in this garden of Eden ... on our island in the sun.

Jack is reading my mind. "You'd miss flying."

"I don't miss anything in the whole universe. Everything I want is right here beside me, in a person named Jack."

After thinking about it, I add.

"Besides, we could have a little Cub parked over there. There's plenty of room for a Cub to take-off along the beach. And this fine sand is packed firm, so she wouldn't sink in. We could build a little palm-thatch shelter for her" ... now I'm really getting carried away ... "right beside the shelter we build for ourselves. We wouldn't need much, just one room, a bed, table, couple of chairs. And a large front porch, with a hammock for two, facing the cove. I'd cook our meals outside on a wood fire. Do you like Oklahoma bar-b-que?"

Jack just smiles, says nothing. He probably doesn't know what it is.

That's one of the many nice things about being with Jack. We can talk, tease each other, play, or just sit together in silence, never feeling a need to talk.

"Race you to the waves." And we go running to the surf, diving into the breakers. Then we sit by the water's edge, side by side, in the soft evening breeze.

"How many stars do you suppose there are up there?" I ask.

"Don't know, but we could count them all. That would take a few weeks, or a few years."

Isaiah has another bonfire going, roasting breadfruit. He carries two warm pieces over to us. "Sorry to be the bearer of unwanted news, but my nephew just ran down the hill to tell me the tower called. Your T-6 is repaired, ready to fly."

Jack looks at me, smiles, then back to Isaiah. "Thanks, friend, we'll be ready to leave at dawn."

I can't resist saying, "I won't be ready to leave at dawn. I won't be ready to leave for a long, long, time, like maybe next month, or the year after next."

Isaiah walks back to the fire, smiling. Jack leans on his elbow, looking into my eyes. I feel the smile I've been wearing for two days disappear at the thought of leaving. "It's too soon, my love, much too soon. Two nights and one day just isn't enough time for two people who have just found their soul mates."

"You know we have to fly those T-6s to Peru. But we'll return here again, soon. I promise."

I know that God made us for each other, so I ask Jack. "You do believe in God, don't you, my love?"

Jack looks out at the stars. "Of course I believe in God. My parents saw to that. They volunteered me to the Episcopal Church for years as an altar boy. I used to wear my football kneepads under my long pants and robe. There was so much kneeling we had to do up there by the altar, especially when the Bishop came, and they got out the incense."

Thinking of big, rugged Jack as a little cherubic altar boy brings a smile to my face. He scratches his chin, turns to look at me, then back skyward.

"Yep, got an early dose of religion. Don't think much about it any more, until something goes wrong that I can't handle, like during the war. Then I promise God I'll never get in such a mess again, if He'll help me out just this once. After He does, I get to thinking, well, that wasn't all that bad, I was just scared. Then I usually go out and do the same dumb things again."

"Jack, my love, you've got to start keeping your promises to God. And stop doing dumb things. Our souls are intertwined now, and I need you around for a long, long, long, time, like forever."

"You're beginning to sound like my brother. He's a Presbyterian minister back in California, and always after me to settle down, raise a family, go to church.

"My church is in the sky. Don't you worry, I'll be around for you. I've got a good reason now, to be a little more careful."

Being so much in love, we decided our passion for physical closeness should wait until after marriage. We found our fun in just being together, getting to know each other, and enjoying the simple pleasures. Like bird watching, strolling hand in hand, watching the sunrise, the sunset. We treasured every minute together, there just weren't enough of them.

Ours was a fairy tale romance come true. We lived every blessed moment to the fullest. Whenever our flight paths crossed, we'd find a few minutes to share our joy.

After delivering a plane to Chile one time, a cable arrived for me in Santiago. "Meet me in New York tomorrow on your way back to Toronto."

We'd hold hands on the Staten Island ferry, fly kites in Central Park, explore the zoo, ride the carousel, just like a couple of kids.

"When you get to Paris wait for me at our crew hotel. I'm on my way," Jack cabled another time.

We would stroll the Left Bank, stopping to kiss, just like Parisian lovers do. We'd climb the Eiffel Tower, the Arch de Triumph. Eat baguettes from the local bakery, dropping crumbs for the birds on the neighborhood sidewalks, as we walked together arm in arm.

Sometimes the cables would read, "I'm waiting for you in London." And we'd play in the fog in Hyde Park, row around the lake, kiss under the weeping willow.

In Argentina we galloped horses along the beach, cooked steaks over an open fire, professed our undying love sitting by the surf, under the Southern Cross.

Between ferry flights we met often, but too briefly. I never had the joy of flying in the same airplane with my beloved.

When Jack flew as a regular line pilot, he lived on the same ten dollars per diem the rest of us did, which had to cover all meals, hotels, laundry, taxis, and everything else. We'd ride airport employee buses, sleep in the cheapest hotels with crew rates, do our own laundry in the bathtub or sink, eat in small neighborhood restaurants. And we went for long walks, enjoying the simple and free pleasures of life.

The other Fleetway pilots noticed the change in us. Gregarious Jack walking off alone to pick wild violets along a taxiway, as he waited to carry my parachute bag and survival gear. Independent me, rushing to hide in his arms as we met on some airport tarmac, walking away to be alone together.

They often said, "The boss has certainly mellowed. He's not chewing us out like he used to. He must be sick. Contagious too. Even Jerrie's acting strange."

Jack's warmth and friendliness made him an excellent Goodwill Ambassador for the United States. Many of the places he flew, he was the first American some had ever seen, and they liked what they saw.

His rugged good looks and gruff manner made him a man's man. And his chivalrous ways endeared him to women. Jack loved to make kids laugh, and was always doing favors for friends and strangers alike. His friends encompassed the globe, always waiting for an opportunity to return his favors.

One time when I was flying out of Bangkok, and Jack out of Jakarta, we met in Malaysia, near Kuala Lumpur. A Malaysian taxi driver friend of Jack's drove us down to the ancient city of Malacca, where we learned the true meaning of "selamat datang." As our dinner was being cooked on hot rocks by the beach, we remembered our cove in Jamaica, and wished upon the stars.

Jack's few faults only made me love him more. He wasn't perfect by any means, only perfect for me. He had his sullen moods, and often was unreasonably stubborn. But heaven knows, I have ten times more faults. Besides, there wasn't a mean bone in his body. Just a few jealous ones.

Jack was a big city boy, born and raised in Los Angeles. Intuitively he always knew the right thing to say, with tenderness and caring. We were totally committed to each other. He was my beloved. He was my best friend.

We drank of deep joy, we laughed with pure delight. We had our seasons in the sun. And in the fog, the rain, the snow. And in the moonlight, and the moonless nights with the stars shining brightly on our world.

No Cinderella ever loved her Prince Charming more.

We found perfect happiness in an imperfect world. Our joy had no bounds. God smiled brightly on us, as we shared many precious moments. Each one a treasure.

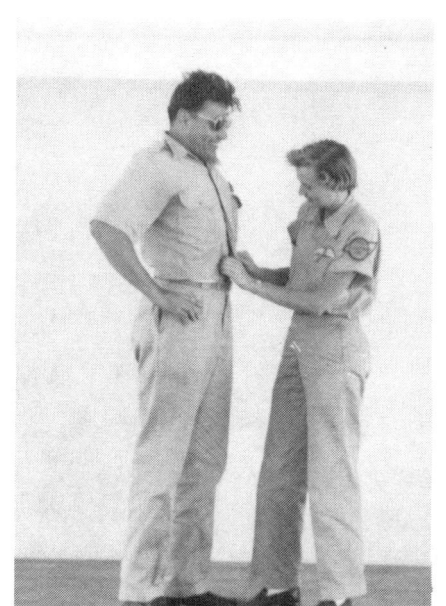

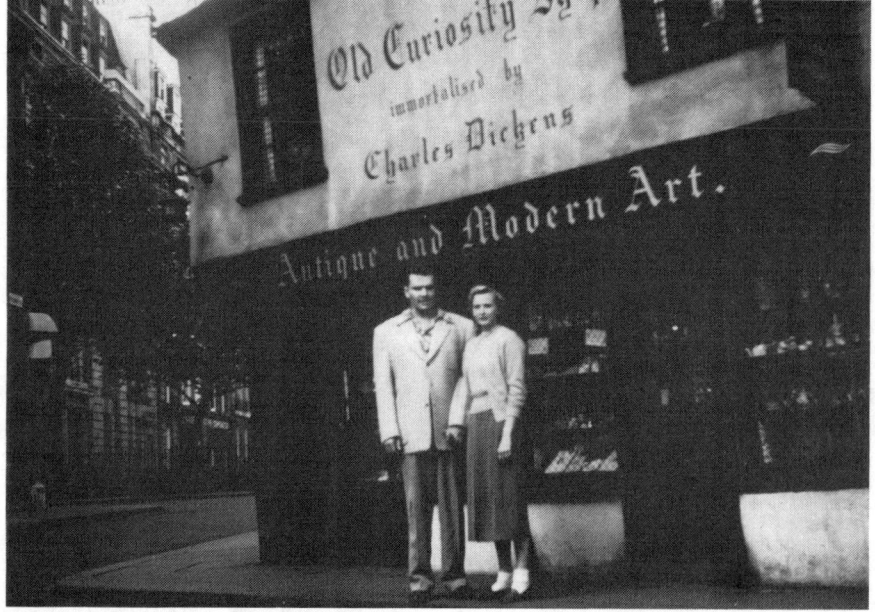

CHAPTER 10

Aero Commander To A World's Altitude Record
Year 1959   Age 28

"... a stall, spiral, or spin, blind in my icy cocoon, is to be averted at all costs."

The stall warning alarm is screaming. I lower the nose just a bit, so as not to lose a single foot of precious altitude. But the urgent alarm keeps screaming ... beep ... beep ... beep ... beep ... beep. It just won't stop.

The choice is clear. Lower the nose some more to build up speed so the airplane won't stall. That means losing some of the precious altitude I've fought so hard to attain, and giving up on my attempt to establish a new World's Record for absolute altitude.

The alternative is to continue fighting for a few more feet to set a new world's record for altitude in this twin-engine aircraft. I am fully aware that my plane can stall any second now, causing her nose to suddenly drop, as well as a wing, putting us into a tight spiral or spin. There would be little hope of recovery, since I have no outside visibility through the ice-coated windows, and I can't trust my frosty instruments.

The thought of my parents and grandmother waiting on the ground flashes through my mind. This is the first time they have been able to watch one of my World Record attempts, and they are excited to be here.

If we stall out, they will watch my plane spinning out of control all the way down from 36,000 feet. Each turn getting tighter, like a corkscrew, until the stress exceeds the design limits of the plane. They will watch the wings and tail section break off, leaving only the fuselage with their daughter, crashing into the ground in front of their eyes. The reporters will ask them, "How does it feel to watch your daughter's airplane spin 36,000 feet down to her death?"

No! I can't subject them to that! My mother and dad would suffer a thousand deaths watching me crash, my grandmother too. No World's Record, nothing, is worth that!

I lower the plane's nose just a little bit more, flying by feel. The stall warning keeps screaming ... beep ... beep ... beep . . . beep. Was there a microsecond delay between those last two beeps, or is it just my wishful thinking? I listen carefully, the beeps ARE hesitating, getting further apart. That means another mile or two safety margin before she stalls.

Aero Commander To
World's Altitude Record

I think back to the beginning of these World Record flights. It has been a long time coming. A year in the planning stage, then another year to set the first two World Records, for maximum speed and maximum distance in this weight category of aircraft. Now I'm about to miss the third and final World Record, absolute altitude.

Oklahoma's bicentennial celebration is this year. My home state is fifty years old, and it is sponsoring these World Record flights in Oklahoma-built twin-engine Rockwell Aero Commanders.

My friend, Ivy Coffey, convinced the State Semi-Centennial Committee to sponsor these World Record attempts with a native Oklahoma pilot. She didn't mention my bashfulness, or that I still get tongue-tied when asked to speak in public.

Ferrying, Fleetway, and Ford, had left me pretty much worn out. Under 100 pounds and exhausted, I returned to the warmth of my family in Ponca City, Oklahoma, for some much needed rest and relaxation. With the tonic of their love, I slowly regained my strength, and started flying again. At first, just little sentimental outings in a borrowed Cub.

When Ivy saw how much it helped me, she became determined to make my long-held dream of setting a World Aviation Record come true. Being a dedicated newspaperwoman, she wasn't about to take "no" for an answer.

Aero Commander To World's Altitude Record

"What's wrong with a woman pilot? Where does it say you have to be a man to fly an airplane? Why, Jerrie's flown all kinds of airplanes, all over the world, has thousands of hours experience. She's flown military fighters, and four-engine bombers. I'm sure she can set new world records in Aero Commanders, built right here in Oklahoma."

Ivy knows nothing about airplanes, loathes flying anywhere. But she knows how much it means to me. She is a true friend.

"Think of all the publicity our State will receive. An Oklahoma girl pilot, young and attractive, flying Oklahoma-built airplanes, setting new World Aviation Records. Breaking the current records set years ago by Russian male pilots in military fighters."

Yes, Ivy is persuasive, and wins sponsorship for me for not one, but three World Aviation Record attempts. The first two I set, for maximum speed and maximum distance, are now official World Records. But I'm about to lose on my absolute altitude attempt.

It's been a long day. Up at dawn to coat the barograph drums with camphor smoke so the stylus can record and confirm the maximum altitude. Then I secured them in their sealed box to the floor of the seven-place Aero Commander, under the watchful eyes of the official judges.

Aero Commander To
World's Altitude Record

Getting into three layers of Air Force arctic clothing took another hour. Forgetting to eat, I started two hours of pre-breathing 100% oxygen to prepare my body for the thin air of high altitude.

Having to use a walk-around oxygen bottle as I pre-flighted the Commander took much longer, and it was almost noon before I finally strapped into the cockpit.

Now, at the hottest time of the day, we're hanging at 36,000 feet in minus forty-five degree cold, just shy of breaking the old Russian altitude record.

"Let's give it one more try to break that record," I'm saying to myself, as well as to my plane. I raise her nose just a hair, and hear the stall warning beeps instantly start increasing.

"Come on now, just a few more feet, that's all we need." Like balancing on a high wire, straining for that ultimate performance, she inches up, one hard-won foot after another.

With both throttles wide open, I adjust her fuel flows for the maximum horsepower that her two Lycoming engines can produce at this altitude. Now it's a battle of weight as she gulps the small supply of avgas remaining on board. With every gallon consumed, she's six pounds lighter. Which translates into a few more feet of altitude.

Running out of fuel doesn't bother me. With all this altitude, it would be no problem to glide down to a dead-stick landing. But a stall, spiral, or spin, blind in my icy cocoon, is to be averted at all costs.

Trying to coax her to climb a few more feet, I play the waiting game, with her dwindling fuel supply. "Go ahead, gulp some more gas, so you can gain a few more feet of altitude."

The stall warning alarm keeps screaming as I hold her smooth and steady so nothing will interfere with the thin air flow over her lifting surfaces at this altitude. If she doesn't run out of airspeed first, she's going to run out of fuel any minute now. This is our last and only chance to set our third World's Record.

Listening carefully to the constant beeps of the stall alarm, I can tell how close we are to stalling by the micro seconds between the beeps. Hoping to get a bit more power from her engines, I fine tune her fuel flows again, and ease her nose back up.

"Come on now, you can do it, just a few more feet, and we'll have it made. Then we can glide back down to the warm earth, and warm embraces."

Poised on the edge, we reach for those last few feet. Another ten, twenty, thirty-five, almost forty feet. That's it, that's all she can do. "Thank you, God."

Aero Commander To
World's Altitude Record

Now she starts shaking, telling me she can no longer fly, the dreaded stall is beginning. Quick, nose down, walk the rudders, let her speed build up so she can start flying again.

I concentrate on keeping her straight with the rudders to stop her from whipping into a spiral or spin. If I can just keep her from spinning until the ice melts off her windows when we hit warmer air...

In a dive now, still unable to see out, I listen to the thin air rushing by. Her engine temperatures are backing down fast now from the never-exceed red lines, with her throttles at idle. "Time to cool off" I tell my plane, "you deserve a little rest, you've earned it."

With a spin narrowly averted, we pull a few "Gs" coming out of the dive at high speed. Then we begin a gentle glide, adding a little power so her engines won't cool down too fast, and warp her cylinders.

Instead of that horrible scene I had visualized my parents watching, we dance and sway, making sweeping circles in the sky, as we descend joyfully back to earth where our loved ones wait.

The ice has melted off the windshields by the time we float down to traffic pattern altitude, allowing us to make a low, high-speed victory pass down the runway.

Midfield we make a sharp pull-up, and circle back to landing, as her engines cough their displeasure with only fumes remaining.

When I open the cockpit door, the hot summer air hits me like a blast from a smelter furnace. The dry bone-chilling cold of high altitude has crept through my layers of arctic clothing, and leaves me shivering in the hot sun.

My ninety-year-old grandmother knows exactly what to do. She sits me down beside her, right on the hot tarmac under the wing, unlaces my fur-lined boots, removes my three layers of wool socks. Then she massages my cold feet with her warm hands.

That works. Soon my shivers are gone, and I begin doing a strip-tease right on the ramp removing all the heavy layers of insulated clothes right down to my flight test jumpsuit.

Mother and Dad wear smiles from ear to ear, and tell me how proud they are of their daughter. I want to celebrate with them, but first I have to remove the sealed barographs, very carefully, so as not to destroy their sensitive recordings on the camphor smoked drums. The officials and judges watch as I place them in special locked wooden containers for them to hand carry back to Washington, D.C. for calibration and confirmation.

Aero Commander To World's Altitude Record

Verified by the National Aeronautic Association, the official results will be sent to France for certification by the Federacion Aeroanutique Internationale as a new World's Aviation Record.

According to my calculations, we have flown higher than anyone before in this aircraft weight category. Several weeks later it is confirmed by the F.A.I. in Paris.

37,010 feet attained by a Rockwell Aero Commander in the U.S.A. has broken the Russian Record set in a YAK II fighter, and is a new World's Record for absolute altitude.

Aero Commander To World's Altitude Record

An Oscar for Oklahoma

THE GIRL: MISS JERRIE COBB, BETHANY, OKLAHOMA. THE AIRCRAFT: AERO COMMANDER 680E. THE ACCOMPLISHMENT: WORLD SPEED RECORD, 2000 KILOMETER COURSE

Aero Commander To
World's Altitude Record

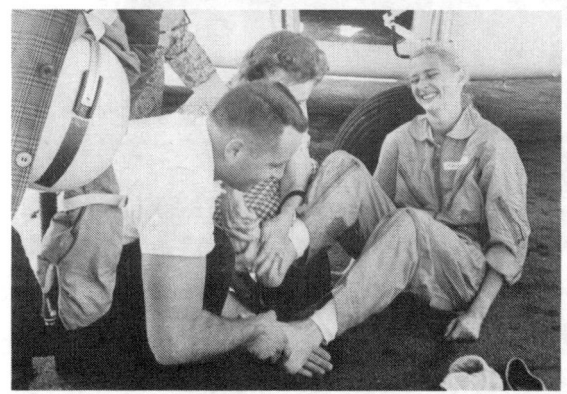

142   Aero Commander To
World's Altitude Record

CHAPTER 11

FLIGHT TO SPACE?
Year 1959-1963   Age 28-32

"Though she competes successfully in a tough masculine trade, 29-year-old Jerrie is a quiet, religious girl with more than the usual pilot's respect for the firmament. She thinks of the sky as "God's unspoiled world which humans should not trespass upon without a feeling of reverence."

Life Magazine
August 29, 1960

ON THE JOB OVER OKLAHOMA CITY, JERRIE COBB DIRECTS TWO OTHER AERO COMMANDER PILOTS IN A ROUTINE FLIGHT TO CHECK NEW RADIO EQUIPMENT

A LADY PROVES SHE'S FIT FOR SPACE FLIGHT

The lady talking on the airplane radio above has just proved an important astronautical point: women are as capable as men of enduring the rigors of space flight. By going through the grueling paces shown in these exclusive LIFE photos Jerrie Cobb of Oklahoma City, U.S. aviation's Woman of the Year for 1959—became the first prospective space pilot in a hitherto unannounced 12-woman testing program being sponsored and conducted by the Lovelace Foundation in Albuquerque, N. Mex.

The secret was let out last week in a technical paper given at an international space symposium in Stockholm by Dr. W. Randolph Lovelace II (below), chairman of NASA's Life Sciences Committee for Project Mercury. Lovelace reported that Jerrie's capacity to withstand the strains of space compared favorably with the men's. Jerrie's test results suggest that female astronauts may even have definite advantages: they have lower body mass, use much less oxygen and need less food, hence may be able to go up in lighter capsules, or stay up considerably longer than men on the same supplies. Their less exposed reproductive system should also give them a higher radiation tolerance. With such favorable results, it now appears inevitable that manned space flight will at some future date become coeducational.

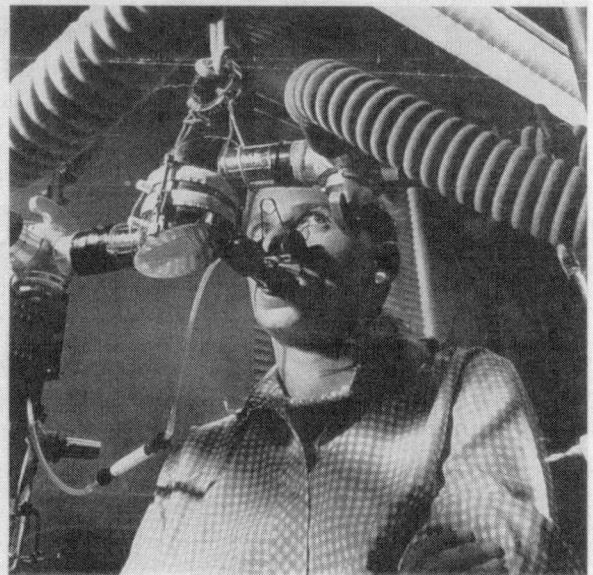

← ORAL EXAM to see how well Jerrie knows her space flight terminology is given by Dr. Lovelace.

PULMONARY FUNCTION TEST measures lung size, detects breathing impairment or obstruction.

Flight To Space?

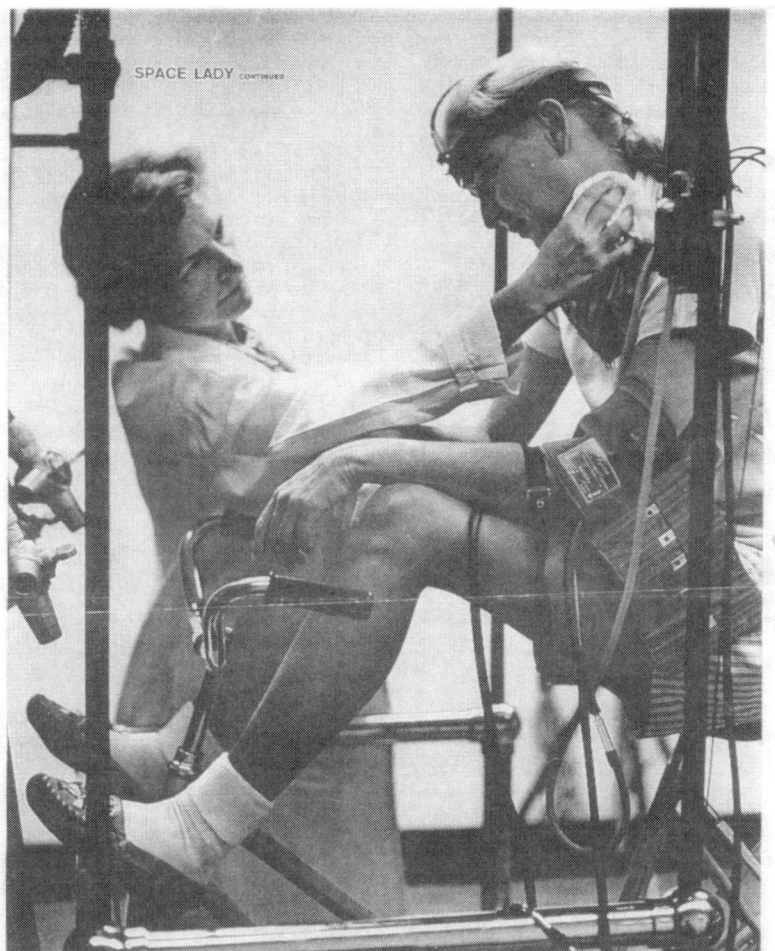

SPACE LADY CONTINUED

PERSPIRING JERRIE IS MOPPED BY LABORATORY RESEARCHER AFTER DEMANDING TEST—10 MINUTES OF HARD NONSTOP PEDALING ON BICYCLE ERGOMETER

AFTER EXHAUSTIVE TESTS, DOCTORS APPROVE

After a series of exhaustive and exhausting medical tests, 75 in all, during which she complained less than the Mercury men had, Jerrie Cobb easily passed the rigid requirements laid down for astronauts-in-training. Jerrie, eager to be the world's first female to go into space, is advertising and sales promotion manager of the Aero Design & Engineering Co., which makes twin-engine Aero Commander planes. A veteran pilot with over 7,500 hours flying a variety of aircraft from crop-dusters to B-17s, she holds world's records for speed, altitude and distance in the twin-engine class. Though she competes successfully in a tough masculine trade, 29-year-old Jerrie is a quiet, religious girl with more than the usual pilot's respect for the firmament. She thinks of the sky as "God's unspoiled world which humans should not trespass upon without a feeling of reverence."

Flight To Space?

TIME, AUGUST 29, 1960

Associated Press
ASTRONAUTRIX COBB
Talent for the trip.

From Aviatrix to Astronautrix

One day last February, trim, 29-year-old Geraldyn Cobb packed a single suitcase, said goodbye to her fellow workers at Aero Design and Engineering Co. in Bethany, Okla., and left for a supposed week's vacation with her parents in Ponca City, 90 miles away. Jerrie Cobb never reached home.

Last week Jerrie's strange disappearance was explained in Stockholm by Dr. W. Randolph Lovelace II, chairman of the Special Committee on the Life Sciences for Project Mercury, the U.S. astronaut program. Jerrie Cobb had spent her "vacation" in Albuquerque, N. Mex. undergoing a brutal battery of 75 separate physical and psychological tests. She was jabbed with an electric needle, rocked back and forth on a tilting table to test her circulation. Her sense of balance was measured by squirting cold water into her ear canals to induce dizziness. Psychologists peppered her with 195 questions (sample: "Do you wish you were dead and away from it all?"), evaluated her ability to adjust to new environments, grasp complicated instructions, keep her sense of humor. The result, according to Dr. Lovelace: she had qualified to "live, observe and do optimal work in the environment of space, and return safely to earth." Jerrie Cobb had become the first U.S. lady astronaut.

Planks on the Pedals. A slender (5 ft. 7 in., 121 lbs.) blonde, Jerrie demonstrated a point that many scientists have long believed: that women may be better equipped than men for existing in space. Reported Project Mercury's Lovelace: women have lower body mass, need significantly less oxygen and less food, hence may be able to go up in lighter capsules, or exist longer than men on the same supplies. Since women's reproductive organs are internally located, they should be able to tolerate higher radiation levels.

The first astronautrix (measurements: 36-27-34) eats hamburgers for breakfast, is an old hand at airplanes, with more air time—over 7,500 hrs.—than any of the male astronauts. The daughter of a then Air Corps captain, Jerrie learned to fly her father's Waco biplane when she was just twelve years old. "Dad fastened 12 in. planks on the pedals so I could reach," she explains.

Guinea Pig. Astronautrix Cobb has no qualms about being a scientific guinea pig, is looking forward to the months of arduous training that will precede her first flight aloft. Next on her rugged schedule: a newly devised, underwater isolation test. Then, in pressure suit and altitude chamber, Jerrie will undergo explosive decompression. She will be whirled about violently in a high-velocity "spinning wheel," seated in an oven-hot chamber, and exposed to dozens of other rigors designed to prepare her for the mental and physical stresses of life in a space capsule. If all goes well, perhaps in late 1962 Jerrie Cobb will don a formless pressure suit, tuck her pony-tail into a helmet and hop atop a rocket for the long, lonely trip into space.

AN AWESOME TEST WAS THE MASTIF, a gigantic device for simulating the pitching, tossing, and tumbling flight possible with an orbiting capsule, which the astronaut must be able to bring under control. MASTIF is the acronym for Multi-Axis Spin Test Inertia Facility.
NASA photo

Flight To Space?

22 Wednesday, Aug. 24, 1960 OKLAHOMA CITY TIMES

Moon Maid's Ready

Flier Shies at Speech, But Lands Her Audience

MISS JERRIE COBB, aviatrix, would rather break another world flight record than make a speech, but last night she stood bravely in front of a microphone.

The 29-year-old blonde folded her arms, took a deep breath and started to tell how

Astronettes? Space Tests a Snap for Jerri

Lady 'Astro'

'Space Lady'

'—And Boy Do I Need a Shave!!'

Now Women Try To Invade Last Male Frontier--Space

Miami Herald

ot To Mention Ho-Ho

Lady In Space? Ha-Ha

By ROBERT C. RUARK

I AM A TOUCH perturbed by the idea that we ... more than a thousa... met one who would...

SCIENCE

No Space For Women

The POWER of FAITH

By Woodi Ishmael

Pretty, pony-tailed Jerrie Cobb has had a fabulous career as a commercial airplane pilot and breaker of world's flying records—something that few women can say.

More recently she has passed tests to qualify her for space flight, has become a consultant to the National Aeronautics and Space Administration, and is a dedicated campaigner for the place of women in our space program.

"With God as my pilot," she says, "I hope to make a space flight."

That is no figure of speech. Faith is a fact in her life—the most important fact! A devout Christian, she attends any church wherever she may be. And amid the turmoil of a banquet or an airfield, you will see her quietly bow her head to say grace.

"God has strong hands which have lifted me high and far," she says.

Flight To Space?

OKLAHOMA CITY TIMES Saturday, May 27, 1961

A happy Jerri Cobb displays her "A OK" certificate declaring her to be "Astronaut of Oklahoma." The Oklahoma City pilot received the citation from James E. Webb, who also named her as a NASA consultant. (AP Wirephoto)

Woman Astronaut Is Down to Earth About Space Flight

By BETTY PEACH

If Jerrie Cobb becomes the first woman space traveler, she may prove to be the most down-to-earth astronaut ever sent into orbit.

Flight To Space?

A veteran pilot at 28, Jerrie Cobb possessed that unique blend of physical toughness and technical skill demanded from the first astronauts.

Flight To Space?

Flight To Space?

Grin and Bear It

"Just think — six months now and not a single Cosmonette!"

"We ought to consider women in our space program gentlemen! . . . If the Russians get ahead of us THAT we'd never hear the last of it!"

HEARINGS

EIGHTY-SEVENTH CONGRESS
JULY 17 AND 18, 1962

Mr. ANFUSO. Miss Cobb, that was an excellent statement. I think that we can safely say at this time that the whole purpose of space exploration is to some day colonize these other planets and I don't see how we can do that without women. [Laughter.]

Now, I think that at this time, Miss Cobb, I would like to insert for the record your qualifications—and your certainly have a great array of achievements.

The biography of Miss Cobb will be inserted in the record.

BIOGRAPHY OF MISS JERRIE COBB

Miss Jerrie Cobb, 31-year-old professional pilot, is considered No. 1 among the announced 13 U.S. women astronaut candidates, by virtue of having undergone and passed 3 separate phases of astronaut testing since February 1960.

Chosen in 1959 as the first woman to undergo the Mecury Astronaut selection tests at Lovelace Foundation, Albuquerque, N. Mex., Miss Cobb completed and passed that battery of 75 physical tests in February 1960.

Following the announcement of her achievement in the summer of 1960 at an international scientific meeting in Stockholm, Miss Cobb next underwent phase II, psychopsychiatric testing, in September 1960 at a Government facility in Oklahoma City, Okla.

The psychological and psychiatric examinations passed included a 9 hour and 40 minutes, record stay in "profound sensory isolation" in water, which tests the subject's mental resources during deprivation of the five basic senses of sight, hearing, taste, feeling and smell while in a simulated weightless environment.

In April 1961 Miss Cobb underwent a 2-week-series of stress tests at the U.S. Navy School of Aviation Medicine, Pensacola, Fla., in a third phase of checking out her mental and psyical capabilities for space flight.

In May of 1961 NASA Administrator James Webb named Miss Cobb a NASA consultant, and she was sworn in the following month in Washington.

Miss Cobb and the 12-woman group who subsequently passed the Lovelace tests last year, have kept in close touch in the effort to bring "lady astronauts" to inclusion in U.S. space efforts.

Miss Cobb, who started flying at the age of 12, has more than 10,000 hours logged, in all types of aircraft. A former international ferry pilot, her ratings include: Commercial license with multiengine, flight instructor, and DC-3 (C-47) captain ratings. Also ground instructor in navigation, meteorology, civil air regulations, aircraft and engines. She has worked as a test pilot and has flown 64 different types of aircraft, including a jet fighter and 4-engine turboprop transport.

Mr. ROUSH. Miss Cobb, I couldn't help but overhear a conversation between you and Mr. Anfuso prior to the hearing and during the course of that conversation you said——

Mr. ANFUSO. I hope you can state this for the record.

Mr. ROUSH. Yes, I can. You said, "I am scared to death." How do you reconcile this emotional statement with the fact that an astronaut must be fearless and courageous and emotionally stable?

Miss COBB. Going up into space couldn't be near as frightening as sitting here. [Laughter.]

Mr. FULTON. So she is automatically excluded unless we eliminate the new rule you and I are speaking about.

Another thing is this:

I believe that the United States should adopt a program of the first woman in space. We should set that as a national goal.

I think for the world it would be a tremendous step forward. While we do have this plan which calls for a race to the moon within this decade, nevertheless I feel that in a program this broad, billions being spent, we should have a first woman in space program, and should state it as a national goal, probably at the highest level, and I would hope that President Kennedy would state such a program.

Would you agree?

Colonel GLENN. I think this is a little out of my province, sir. [Laughter.]

Flight To Space?

Mr. FULTON. Come, come. How about Commander Carpenter?

Commander CARPENTER. I think maybe the question would better be, When should we do this? I disagree with you that this is only a new area that we will all soon travel in. I think at this time it is definitely an experiment. There are many unknowns and it is important for us to eliminate as many of these unknowns before the flights take place as is possible.

Mr. FULTON. Yes, but, you see, doesn't that lead you into the old question of protecting women? And to me it sounds as if we are going to protect women in the kitchen, on the ground and in the home. We do not want them to get out where things are exciting, or have adventure, where there might be risks.

Commander CARPENTER. No, I believe it is protecting our program.

Mr. FULTON. Against women?

Commander CARPENTER. No, sir; not against women.

Mr. ANFUSO. If the gentleman will yield. Wouldn't you say, Commander Carpenter, that you are protecting women by letting men do the daring first, and when the trip to the moon, or any place else, becomes less hazardous, then we would take the other position; is that

> Mr. FULTON. I disagree basically on your approach, because I believe that space is not an experiment or adventure. I think it is a new area where everybody will operate.
> Under those circumstances, when women are paying the taxes here, as much or more than the men, I don't think they should be kept out of space because of rigid requirements.

Secondly, in 1959 there were the Lovelace Foundation tests at Albuquerque, N. Mex., 75 physical tests were completed in February 1960 by Miss Jerrie Cobb. Miss Cobb and this 12-woman group passed these tests.

Then Miss Cobb underwent the 2-week series of tests at the U.S. Navy School of Aviation Medicine in Pensacola in April 1961, and passed.

Then what happened?

In May of 1961 Administrator James E. Webb names Miss Cobb a NASA consultant. So she holds a position and says what is to be done but is not allowed to do it. She is not allowed to participate.

Now, my feeling is this. Since this group of women has passed these tests successfully, NASA should outline a training program that does not interfere with the current programs but will let women participate.

If I could finish with this, Mr. Chairman: It is the same old thing cropping up, where men want to protect women and keep them out of the field so that it is kept for men.

I feel that we should equally be in a race with Russia to place the first woman in space.

I think that would be a clear first, as much as landing on the moon—to me, it would be more.

Colonel GLENN. I think this gets back to the way our social order is organized, really. It is just a fact. The men go off and fight the wars and fly the airplanes and come back and help design and build and test them. The fact that women are not in this field is a fact of our social order. It may be undesirable.

Slipping off her shoes, Miss Jerrie Cobb (left) gets in stride as she testifies before a House space subcommittee on the issue of selecting women as astronauts in the space program. Beside her is another witness, Mrs. Janey Hart, wife of Sen. Philip Hart of Michigan. (AP Wirephoto)

Courage Tested

Space Heroes Put on Spot

WASHINGTON (UPI)—Government space officials got a chance Wednesday to say whether they really stacked the regulations against woman astronauts and if so, why.

The two most famous United States space travelers —Col. John H. Glenn jr., and Cmdr. M. Scott Carpenter —also were put on the spot.

Flight To Space?

U.S. Space View
It's for Men Only

Jerrie Cobb Wishes She Had Won Space Race

By Joy Miller

NEW YORK, June 18 (AP)—
FOR THREE YEARS Jerrie Cobb has harangued, lectured and pleaded that women belong in space as much as men.

Now the Russians have put a woman in orbit, but it's a bittersweet victory for Jerrie.

In the first place, the first woman astronaut is not an American, and in the second, she's not Jerrie.

The blond Oklahoma pilot, first woman to pass the rigorous tests given the astronauts, for years has lived in hope of being the first woman in space. Now she says in a telephone interview.

I really mean it when I wish her well, Godspeed and a good flight. I'm glad a woman made it. But I'm sorry she's not an American.

JERRIE COBB

Jerrie: 'We Could Have Done It'

SCIENCE

No Space For Women

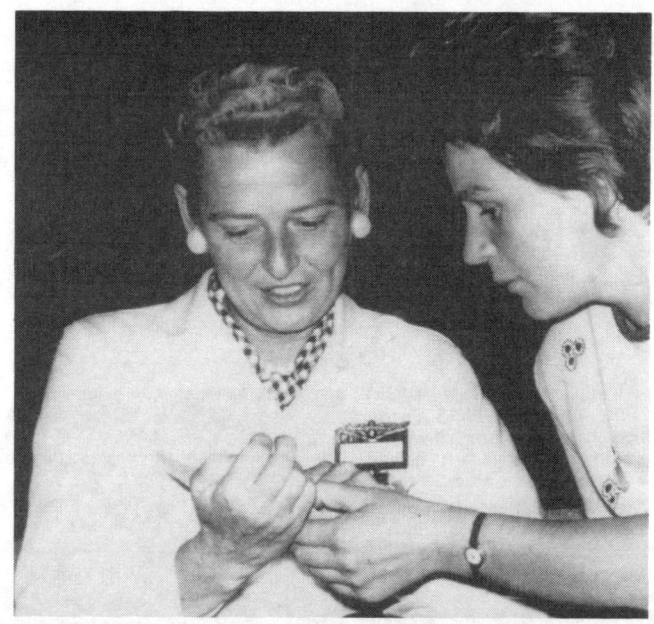

In Mexico with the first woman and the first man to fly in Space, Valentina Tereshkova and Yuri Gagarin from Russia.

Flight To Space?   159

160 **Flight To Space?**

BOOK IV

Flying In The Amazon Jungle Of South America

12. Juliet Charlie To Amazonas
    Year 1963   Age 32   page 163
    Jamaica
    Juliet Charlie
    Flight to Amazonas

13. Juliet Charlie To The Rio Putamayo
    Year 1965   Age 34   page 179
    Jungle rain, landing
    Indigenous culture
    Maloca life, and death

14. Juliet Charlie To The Amazon Headwaters
    Year 1969   Age 38   page 193
    Radio message, celebrating
    Amazon jungle flying
    Jungle landing

15. Shamans Fly To The Moon
    Year 1969   Age 38   page 207
    Tribal greeting
    Moon landing, no surprise
    Wingtop moon talk

CHAPTER 12

Juliet Charlie To Amazonas
Year 1963   Age 32

"Within each of us is a spark that wants to shine, to contribute to something larger than self."

The thrill of flying in jungle skies is not what is luring me to Amazonas. It's the indigenous people, the beauty of the rain forest, the desire to be useful, that's attracting me to the jungle. My spiritual journey is leading me to Amazonas, in search of ways to express the joy in my heart.

No one really understands. My family thinks I just want to be alone, after the disappointment of not getting to fly in space. My friends think I'm being foolish. Some think I'm running away to hide. Others say I'm just an itinerant "do-gooder," as if that's a bad word.

My peers think I'm throwing away a fine flying career. "How can you even think of going off to fly in some far-away jungle? You worked hard, against overwhelming odds, to get to the top in aviation. You've earned all the big awards, Pilot Of The Year, Top Woman Pilot, Amelia Earhart Achievement Medal, Gold Wings of the Federación

Aeronautique Internationale. You're a four-time World Aviation Record holder, test pilot, almost astronaut. Now you're offered top management jobs in aviation. How can you possibly think of throwing it all away, just to fly off to some dreary jungle?"

I try to explain that there are more important things in life to me than just earning a living, just being successful in my chosen line of work. Besides, my successes are not my own, the way to them was prepared by others, who sacrificed much. I owe a debt of gratitude to Amelia Earhart, Louise Thaden, Charles Lindberg, and other fliers who came before me.

Nothing that I accomplished was done alone. The talent and abilities given me, like my health and genes, were neither earned nor chosen. They are gifts, given not so much for the joy they bring me, but to share with others. If I bury my flying talent in some executive suite, it is wasted and lost forever. If I use it to serve the isolated, primitive peoples of Amazonas, it lives on.

When the Congressional Hearings ended I felt lost. The two most important parts of my life, Jack, and flying in space, had been denied. I need to be alone, separate, away from everything, to figure out what to do with the rest of my life. Not even the warmth of my loving family can help this time.

A very private cove in Jamaica calls to me. At this lowest ebb of my life, I need to be back where I have been the happiest in my life.

A kind Jamaican family rents me a one-room thatched hut where I can read, sleep, think, watch the breakers, dream, and be alone. The type of hide-a-way I had dreamed of sharing with Jack.

Jamaicans are usually gregarious people, but instinctively know when one needs to be alone. They often bring me fruit, exchange pleasantries, but never stay to chat.

For days I walk the beach, deep in thought, praying, pleading.

"Why, Lord, did you take away the two most important parts of my life?

"Why did you let me waste three precious years of my life preparing to be an astronaut if they weren't going to let a woman fly in space?"

It all pours out. The thought occurs to me of spending the rest of my life in this hut. Living as a hermit hidden away from society, happy in my self-imposed solitude. It's an enticing idea. But Jack was right, I would miss flying too much.

Slowly, life comes back into focus. I could never be happy living for myself alone. We are here to help one another.

Life is a gift, as is love, given to us to share. The freedom of the sky that I crave is a gift also, freely given. God overwhelms us with gifts, and all He asks of us is to love one another. He is our

Father, and he has a very large family. Within each of us is a spark that wants to shine, to contribute to something larger than self.

Before my three years of training for space flight, I had thought about becoming a missionary pilot. When I wrote to three mission groups, I was told, "Only men serve as pilots on the mission field. Women serve as wives, mothers, nurses, teachers." Since flying is my life, and I don't fit into any of those other categories, I gave up the idea.

Now I'm thirty-two and wondering what to do with the rest of my life. The only thing I'm sure of, is that somehow I want to find a way of expressing my thankfulness for all that's been given me. And since I'm not very good with words, it will have to be with actions.

No longer am I content to be the receiver of all things good without showing my gratitude to the Giver of all things good. No longer am I comfortable living on this beautiful planet Earth, taking up space, breathing her air, drinking her water, without contributing to her welfare.

Since the ultimate source of our gifts and talents is God, I want to give as a gift what I have received as a gift. Somehow I need to find a way of using my life, my flying, in serving others.

I think about the Amazon jungle in South America. How people, governments, international companies are destroying the rain forest, just to make a quick profit. Thousands of acres of pristine jungle are being burned every day, destroying the valuable plants and animals forever. It's happening during my watch on Earth, therefore I am responsible.

Plants are the first link in all of life, our basic life support system here on Earth. They feed us, clothe us, heal us, effect our entire life cycle. And they're being burned in the jungle before we even know what good they hold for us. Perhaps if I could fly people over the jungle so they can see the terrible harm being done, it might help stop the burning of that magnificent corner of creation.

I wonder how I can learn about Amazonas, the most isolated living area in the world. More days I spend walking the beach, thinking, praying. Until the answer becomes obvious. As important as it is to help preserve the rain forest, people are still more important. After all, primitive man is the most endangered species on earth.

Perhaps the indigenous people of Amazonas would teach me about their jungle home. By serving them, maybe I can help preserve their rain forest home. That's when I know I'm being led to the mission field, even though I resist it all the way.

"You know I tried before, Lord, the mission groups don't want me. Not as a pilot, and that's the talent you've given me. It's the same as in the space program, the flying jobs are reserved for men only.

"There's no way I can be a missionary, I enjoy earthly pleasures too much.

"I have a hard time talking with friends about you, much less strangers. You gave me the gift of flying, not talking, and that's the way I like it.

"You made me, you know I'm not pious, not missionary material.

"You know I'm not religious enough to be a missionary. Not worthy."

In spite of my protests, the answer doesn't change.

"Go, ... I am with you always."

It's hard to say "no" to someone who won't leave you alone. And God isn't interested in my excuses.

Before the month is out I've left my idyllic cove for the most remote area of the world, the Amazon jungles of South America. There I volunteer my flying talent on the mission field.

The few missionary groups serving in the jungle are polite about it, but still nobody wants me. A thirty-two-year-old experienced pilot with thousands of flying hours in all kinds of airplanes, flying all over the world, is not welcome in the mission field. Wrong gender. They want their pilots straight out of bible school with a brand new commercial license, 200 hours total flying time. And only males need apply.

Juliet Charlie To Amazonas

For the second time rejected, I know I'll have to do it alone, solo, like everything else in my life. All I need is God, and an airplane.

Back in the States I find a neglected twin Aero Commander in an Arkansas pasture for sale cheap. The problem is, I have no money. Three years of paying my own expenses traveling around the country for NASA in the space program drained my savings. And I spent the last of my "emergency fund" on the trip to the missionary bases in South America .

My parents will never understand why in the world I want to go to some far-off jungle to fly as a missionary pilot. But it is my dad who volunteers to co-sign the note at the First National Bank of Ponca City, Oklahoma, so that they will lend me the money to buy the broken-down Commander.

After two weeks camping out in the Ozark pasture, I finally get her cleaned up and flyable, with her new F.A.A. registration number painted in purple on her fuselage, N-12JC. Since all letters are spoken as words in aviation, she becomes November-One-Two-Juliet-Charlie, or Juliet for short.

She needs a lot more work, but first we have to earn some money to make her bank payments, and pay for the parts she needs. Before heading for the jungle we also need a cash reserve to buy spares and fuel. So Juliet and I have an understanding. We will earn our keep by flying, at whatever we can find, as long as we can do it together.

We start out by flying lobsters, or crayfish as the Bahamians call them, from the Out Islands of the Bahamas to Miami. Alive and wiggling, they are put into large plastic trash cans, and loaded in Juliet for the island-hopping flights. It leaves us smelling a little fishy, but it pays for the parts she needs, and makes her bank payments.

Juliet and I become real beach bums. Camping out on Little Andros Island in the Bahamas at night is far cheaper than renting a place in Miami, and much more fun. The living is easy, and the flying is great. Just what we need, good tonic for both of us.

Flying low and slow between the islands in beautiful weather, I admire the abundant marine life of the Great Bahama Bank. From my lovely perch above the sea it's easy to spy on teeming schools of fish, and bottle-nose dolphins playing with their young. Often we swoop down and circle the playful porpoises, following along like one of the group. The clear water also reveals circling sharks, green turtles, and occasionally a lost whale. What a delight to watch these beauties of the sea from my magic carpet named Juliet.

Everyday we start the lobster run shortly after sunrise, stopping at several Out Islands among the more than eight hundred in the Bahamas, until our load is complete. Then we fly across the Gulf

Stream, landing at my favorite big airport, Miami International, usually around noon.

After clearing customs and unloading the lobsters, we often taxi over to "corrosion corner" where all the old junked airplanes are parked. There I scrounge around for any used parts I can find to clean up and rebuild to use for Juliet. Bit by bit we're accumulating the spares we'll need in the jungle.

By late afternoon we're winging back over the Gulf Stream playing among the towering cumulus. In the long summer evenings I happily work on Juliet, making sure every part of her is clean and in perfect working order. At night I lie in my hammock strung under her wing and watch the stars in the tropical sky, dreaming of our future life in the jungle.

It's easy living, beautiful flying, fun work. Just what we need to get ready to fly south. It fills our need to keep up with Juliet's bank payments and buy her repair parts. By the end of lobster season we have an assortment of spares, all our bills are paid, and enough left to buy fuel for our first few months of jungle flying.

There's no one to wave us off, but it's a happy day when we finally take off for the jungle of South America, Juliet and I, to serve the indigenous people of Amazonas. How we are going serve them I'm not really sure. But life is a spiritual adventure and sometimes we have to just start out, to find the answers.

The flight across the Caribbean is calm and peaceful, with the usual altocumulus clouds to weave around. It's a different story when we hit the Intertropical Convergence Zone lying just offshore the northern coast of South America. Extending hundreds of miles from east of Venezuela to west of Panama, there is no way around. We have to fly through, hoping we can avoid the embedded thunderstorms.

Juliet doesn't carry radar to show us where the most violent cells are located, so we sort of pick and choose our way, trying to stay in the lighter gray areas, and out of the dark heavy rain.

Flying alone in Juliet I think of how vulnerable we are, a tiny feather over the ocean, being tossed to and fro by nature's storms. Enveloped in the clouds, concentrating on the instruments, we turn first one way, then another, trying to thread our way between the heavy cells. Better to be off course, than pounded with hail.

When it gets so dark I have to turn the instrument lights up to high intensity in the middle of the day I know it's time to turn back. The heavy rain, and severe turbulence is more than Juliet can take.

There's a lighter grey area to the east, not the black clouds we've just been in, so we turn towards it. The rain becomes lighter, and the bouncing less severe. We may be off course, but we're threading our way through, by trial and error.

Strange to think that just the degree between light and dark grey can sometimes be the difference between life and death. Surrounded by rain-soaked clouds, I think of the frailness of human life. I tend to forget about the results of poor judgement in the sky, where something as simple as turning right instead of left, can sometimes destroy lives.

Flying is a lonely occupation, which suits me fine. Living so close to the edge makes me think a lot about what's really important in life. Certainly not how long we live, or how much money we make. Maybe it's the little things that are important. Like sharing laughter, helping friends, smelling flowers. Or the large things, like the star-filled sky, the glorious sunrise, the love of family, friends.

Yes, it's definitely a lighter grey here. And over to the left, around that dark area. Back and forth we pick and choose, weaving our way through the heavy line of storms, as through life.

Suddenly, without warning, we break out into the clear, with the coast of South America visible on the horizon. Cartagena, Colombia never looked so pretty, as in the after-rain amber light of the late afternoon sun.

After a restful overnight, we're off at dawn to cross the Magdalena River flood plain, then the Andes Mountains, eagerly heading for the largest jungle in the world.

Flying over the flood plain of northern Colombia in soft early morning purple light I'm thinking maybe I take life too seriously. Perhaps it's enough just to be alive, to live each day to the fullest, to be grateful for this marvelous gift of life. But how do we express our thankfulness, if not by serving others? Certainly the only thing that lives on after us is the love we give to others, that part of ourselves that we give away.

Looking down on the Magdalena River as it sweeps through the lowlands I can see miles of networks of dikes still standing after more than a thousand years. They were made by Pre-Columbian people of the Sinu culture to cultivate their crops, when they lived on this flood plain for 500 years, ending a thousand years ago.

They were an enterprising people, trading with other great American civilizations, rivaling those of Europe and Asia at the time. The Incas to the south. The Mayans and Aztecs to the north. The Taironas to the East.

When they built the dikes they found gold washed down from the Andes, and fashioned it into intricate ornaments to wear for celebrations, and to bury with their dead. The gold-working techniques they developed were far superior to any other in the world at that time, and collections of their gold work are still much admired in museums today.

One of the many joys of flying in remote areas of the world is to find such ancient and beautiful monuments of once grand cultures. From the ground they're difficult to notice, but from the sky, they stand out in all their former grandeur.

The Andes Mountains loom ahead. We have to cross them before the heat of the day sends towering clouds to perch among the peaks. Since Juliet is outfitted for low jungle flying, we have to cross these high mountains at their lowest point. By most gauges the Andes are the mightiest mountain range in the world. The Himalayas have the highest peak, but the Andes range is longer, and contains many more peaks above 20,000 feet.

Just south of a snow-capped peak on the Caribbean coast called Sierra Nevada de Santa Marta is a lower ridge we can skim across on a clear day. I start looking for it, find it, head for it, happy it's not blocked by clouds this morning. Just as we approach the first ridge around 8,000 feet we hit some downdrafts and have to turn back, circle, and climb up higher.

It's bumpy as we finally cross over the ridge at about 9,000 feet. Now we're knowingly trapped, surrounded by mountains with peaks on all sides up to 18,000 feet, much higher than Juliet can fly. But I know we can escape by skimming across a few lower ridges between the high peaks on a clear day. We squirm our way around one peak, over another ridge, right, left, making sure not to get into any clouds. Around here they conceal very high mountain tops.

Threading our way through the Andes I admire the beautiful greenery everywhere. The mountains are covered with lush tropical growth, waterfalls, roaring rivers descending steep slopes in crashing flumes, reflecting rainbows in the sun.

After all these years I'm still enchanted by this wonderful gift of flying. Just to be able to see these marvels of nature, these beautiful sights reserved for the birds, and the few who fly, is a great delight. I often wish for better words to describe the sheer beauty, and my gratitude for the gift of flying that allows me to see it.

After about three hours I see a large verdant plain just beyond the last tall peak. Crossing over its base at 11,000 feet I marvel at the vast prairie, the grassy plains of the llanos, stretching as far as eye can see. A lighter green than the Andes, this enormous savanna covers more than 120,000 square miles, from the base of the Andes until the jungle takes over the landscape.

The tall-grass land of the llanos gives a little respite between the world's mightiest mountains and the world's mightiest jungle in Colombia and Venezuela. Further south in Ecuador and Peru the jungle creeps all the way up into the foothills of the Andes.

Juliet Charlie To Amazonas

Juliet and I glide down to have some fun exploring the rivers and small patches of gallery forest running through the llanos. We circle a flock of roseate spoonbills feeding along a river, and see small deer feeding in the grass. We discover there are gently rolling hills under the tall grass, and it's all as green as a well fertilized golf course.

We make another stop to refuel at a small strip in the llanos, a missionary base of the Wycliffe Bible Translators, called Lomolinda for the pretty hills that surround it. Then we're off again for our destination, the center of the Amazon jungle.

As we fly further south, the patches of gallery forest get larger and more numerous, until they become one gigantic jungle, spreading over our entire world. Now we're surrounded by dense jungle, over two million square miles covered with trees, an area bigger than the entire United States.

Intrigued by the ocean of trees below us, Juliet and I swoop down to get a closer look. These are majestic trees, some towering over others, and occasionally a giant tree whose canopy covers all those around it.

So dense is the tangle of trees that I can't see the jungle floor 200 or more feet below the tree tops. But I can see the profusion of flowers reaching for the sun, and the brightly colored birds. Scarlet macaws, blue and yellow macaws, military macaws, circling around the tree tops, and channel-bill toucans looking for a branch in the sun. It's so much fun watching the bright and lively birds that we stay low to enjoy our private exotic bird show.

There are only a few patches of rain sweeping over the jungle this afternoon, which we easily fly around. Except for a little shower we fly through to wash the sea salt off Juliet from her ocean crossing, so her aluminum skin won't corrode.

Getting more excited by the mile, we count off the hours until we reach the mightiest river of them all, 4,000-mile-long Rio Amazonas.

A small port town on the grand river, Leticia is our destination because it's about in the center of this overwhelming jungle. It is on the Colombian side, but Peru is just across the big river, and Brazil is only a short hike away.

Climbing just a little to look for the great river, I can see her now, stretching across the horizon from one end to the other. She looks more like a long lake that goes on forever. I'm only beginning to grasp the enormity of this land.

More foolish than brave, we're headed straight for the heart of the largest rain forest on earth. After circling low over the small port town a thousand miles up the Rio Amazonas, Juliet lightly sets down on the muddy strip. "Thank you, God."

Like a kid having trouble waiting her turn, my blood is simmering to fly in these Amazonas skies. But first we have to learn about living in the jungle, about serving others. And the only way I learn is the hard way, by doing it.

CHAPTER 13

Juliet Charlie To The Rio Putamayo
Year 1966   Age 35

*"Life is a spiritual thing,
and spiritual things are simple."*

    Rainy season has descended on this part of mid-Amazonas in all its fury. Juliet and I are flying in heavy rain, trying to reach a small indigenous tribe living on a creek just upriver of the Rio Putamayo.

    The urgent message arrived too late in the day for us to leave yesterday. Several of my indigenous friends had walked and paddled for three days to ask the Bishop of Amazonas to send me a radio message in the Peruvian area of Amazonas, hundreds of miles away, where I've been flying the past few months. Their chief is dying, and they asked if I could come to their communal house, their maloca.

    Juliet and I took off just before dawn, climbing blindly up through the low stratus clouds still hanging in the trees after a big rainstorm during the night.

The fog doesn't burn off as usual after sunrise, because the sun is buried behind several more layers of rain-soaked clouds above. We fly for four hours, holding a constant heading plotted on my hand-made maps.

Time and distance is the only means of navigation since the poor visibility prevents us from seeing the single river checkpoint to confirm our speed and position. The solid clouds above us and broken ones below us are growing thicker and merging, pushing us ever lower towards the trees.

It's raining again, getting heavier and darker the farther we fly. Trying to keep some visual reference with the trees we're forced down to almost their level. Now we're flying about 200 feet above the Rio Putamayo, twisting and turning with every bend in the river. Looking for the mouth of the creek that will lead us to the one-way strip near their maloca, where the tribe lives communally under one large thatched roof.

Juliet is purring steadily along, but I'm getting anxious. It's my own fault for not turning back when we still had enough fuel to make it back. Now we are committed, there are no other alternatives, we have to find the short strip within minutes, or land in the river. The clouds are in the trees, pouring rain everywhere. The visibility is less than the width of the river.

We should have been there four minutes ago. We turn back, barely skimming the agitated water, flying upriver now. Minutes tick off. There's something ahead. No, just some trees down. But what's that over there? Yes, that's it, the creek!

Hard right rudder.
We're too fast, slow her down ... more.
Gear down, locked, pressure up.
There's the strip now, turn in fast, steeper.
Don't lose sight of it, this is our only chance.
Slow her down some more ... more.
Full flaps.
The wind's blowing us off, lower the wing.
Keep her straight, opposite rudder.
Props forward, fuel boosts on.
Hang on, we're going in.
Straighten up, more rudder.
SQUISH, SQUISH

We're down, rushing at sixty mph towards the trees at the end of the short wet strip. Juliet's brakes are useless as we slide on a sea of red mud splashing in all directions, covering the windshield, blinding us.

I sit in Juliet clutching her control yoke to my breast, trying to keep her rudder pedals even, wondering when we will hit the first trees. Finally her big wheels sink in, and the mud yanks us to an abrupt stop, as quickly as the arresting cable on an aircraft carrier.

There stand my friends in all their innocence, purity, and dignity. Waiting in the pouring down rain, naked and cold. They greet us with wet hugs and sad eyes, thanking us for coming.

They unload my knapsack and hammock while I grab a box of medicines and wrap it in my rain poncho. We put Juliet's control locks on quickly, refueling will have to wait this time.

We start down the jungle trail, which is now a small stream in the jungle rain. We're headed for their maloca where the sick ones wait in their hammocks. I've walked this long trail many times, mostly during happier times.

I think of all the trails I've walked with my indigenous friends the past three years. Sharing the communal life of these gentle people, I've learned how to trot along their jungle trails, keeping an eye out for snakes, while hunting for food with a blowgun.

They've also taught me how to paddle a dugout canoe, with only an inch or two of freeboard, through river rapids without ending up in the water, as piranha bait. And how to plant and prepare their staple crop, cassava, being careful to strain out all the poison. Every day has been a new learning experience. They began by teaching me the basics of surviving in the jungle

"Never go out after dark.

"Hunt for food in groups of two or three, quietly."

"Bathe in a creek with running water, once or twice a day, in groups."

"Live communally, sharing, helping, caring for each other."

There's always something new to learn. Jungle weather patterns, wind systems, violent storm paths. Languages, Spanish and Portuguese, but more important, tribal tongues, since my new friends speak only their own unwritten languages.

There are no accurate maps of Amazonas because her many clouds prevent aerial photography. Making my own maps has been a long and hard learning experience. So far, they've kept us from getting lost in this enormous land with no radio or navigational aids to guide us. But I'm constantly making corrections.

It's a full time job sketching out maps of the river systems, and the few distinguishing features in this ocean of trees. Sometimes I add a giant tree I haven't noticed before, which can be used for a wind and ground speed check. Or a small lake forming from an old riverbed, after the river has carved a new path through the jungle. Or a new maloca of indigenous people not seen before.

My hand-drawn maps are my most important possession, for without them I would be lost in the jungle. I keep them in plastic covers to protect them from the rain, and update them on every flight. My life depends on their accuracy.

I hesitate to call myself a missionary, since I still don't fit the mold. But if a missionary is a person on a mission, then we qualify. Because we certainly have a mission, Juliet and I. To show that a very ordinary person, and a somewhat battered airplane, can be used by God to help these isolated people.

The past three years couldn't have been happier for me. Blessed with the friendship of these gentle people, surrounded by the absolute beauty of the rain forest, having the privilege of flying in spectacular jungle skies, makes my heart sing with joy.

Often we are flying sunup to sundown since we offer our jungle airlift service to missionaries of all faiths, as well as the indigenous people. The Bishop of Amazonas was the first to accept, never once questioning my piloting ability, gender, sincerity, religious beliefs, or reason for being here. We have a friendly, simple agreement. He supplies the gas. I supply the airplane. And off we go, flying in jungle skies, serving the indigenous people.

The Bishop is a delightful fellow, a true man of God, with a marvelous sense of humor. There is much I could learn from him if we could only

Juliet Charlie To The Rio Putamayo

converse on a deeper level. He spent years studying at the Vatican and speaks seven languages fluently, but, alas, English is not one of them. My Spanish and Portuguese are still poor, and I'm still learning the tribal tongues.

Because Christopher Columbus was looking for the Far East Indies, and assumed he had found them, he named the inhabitants that welcomed him to the Americas, "Indians."

The ancestors of my friends did not come from India or the East Indies. They are not "Indians." Eons ago their forefathers may have come across the land bridge from Asia to Alaska, and migrated south. Or maybe they came across the Pacific on rafts, Kon-Tiki style. But it was all a very long time ago, because their forefathers have lived here since before 10,000 B.C. They have every right to be called Americans.

They are the native people of the Americas, and some of the finest examples of human kindness in the world today. Indeed, I consider it an privilege to call them my friends.

Like people throughout the world, their languages are very important to them. Sometimes their language is all they have left of a once grand culture. They teach me their tongues in confidence, and I never use them outside of the tribes to which they belong.

Like most school subjects, language learning comes hard for me. I'm still working on Spanish and Portuguese. But the tribal languages are easier for me to learn. The indigenous people don't have a need for a lot of words. We get along fine.

Actually it doesn't take long at all to learn a tribal tongue. Living in a maloca for a few months will give you the basics. The kids are the best teachers, at least they have the most patience with my many mistakes. They giggle at my mispronouncing and tease me, but they make sure I get it right.

They call Juliet "the Bird" in their tongue, and are always happy to hear her coming. Their ears can recognize the sound of her engines more than forty miles away. The men leave their hunting, the women their cassava fields, to run to their strip to greet us.

This normal half-hour hike to their maloca takes over an hour today on the rain slick trail. We are drenched, but the medicine keeps dry, wrapped in my plastic poncho.

There's one thing to say about living without clothes in the jungle. It sure is easier to dry off. Their naked bodies are already dry, while I'm still getting out of my wet clothes in a dark corner of the maloca, leaving a mud puddle on the dirt floor. Hanging my rain-soaked jeans over my hammock rope, they continue to drip, piddle, paddle, into the puddle.

Juliet Charlie To The Rio Putamayo

My dry clothes are helping to warm me up as I walk over to where the women are gathered around the cooking fire. They offer me some hot water to drink, and I add a portion of rice, and some precious salt, to their cooking pot. In the large ceramic pot, made from river mud, simmers a soup of cassava and plantains for all who are able to eat.

The chief lies in his hammock, in a coma. In the midst of a meningitis epidemic, he is dying of the disease, one never known in the jungle until the white man came.

He is very dear to me. He was among the first of the indigenous people I met when we first arrived in Amazonas three years ago, knowing nothing about the people, or the jungle. He welcomed me warmly when I arrived at this maloca one stormy late afternoon, feverish and alone, in a dugout canoe half filled with water. His tribe fed me, housed me, treated my malaria, taught me their language, and invited me to live with them. He is like a big brother to me, and has taught me much.

One day I asked him about the romantic notion of "the noble savage" living happily alone and unbothered in his jungle paradise. He told me that's not the way it really is. He said they lived in terrible fear, more of evil spirits, than jaguars and anacondas, and that they welcomed change in their lives.

He said they wanted to learn to grow something besides cassava in their jungle home, so they wouldn't have to hunt daily for meat, which was getting harder to find in this part of the jungle. He said they would appreciate any help at all, that the neighboring tribes had similar problems, and there was no one to help any of them.

Their shaman told me he needed more medicines because the people were often sick, and many died early in life, especially the babies and youngsters. Like people the world over, they wanted a better life for their children.

Juliet and I brought them seeds to grow more nourishing crops. Antibiotics, vaccines, to treat their many illnesses. Anti-venom for their snake-bites.

As I learned more of their language, there were words in their tongue for "the Spirit who created the sky." I reminded them that the same Spirit created each of us, and is stronger than all the evil spirits.

Their chief was a fine young leader of his people. With the seeds we brought, he showed them how to improve their diet with nourishing food, saving half the seeds to replant, and share with other tribes. At harvest time they would invite every tribe within a day's paddle to a big feast in celebration of "the Spirit who created the sky."

They learned that they do not have to live in fear of any man or evil spirit. That as children of "the Spirit who created the sky" we are all made with dignity and worth. That they do not have to fear death, their soul to be eaten by some huge snake, or left to roam the jungle, forever homeless. They know "the Spirit who created the sky" loves all that He has made, and will never leave us, even in death.

I learned how much we all need to be looked after, cared for. That dogma is not as important as love. That caring for each other, serving one another, brings joy to our hearts.

We know that life is a spiritual thing, and spiritual things are simple. Spirituality is at the very heart of our being. Our lives are saturated with spiritual values for the spirit of our Creator is present is all creation. It's a wonderful and humbling experience to live in a maloca full of mystics.

They treat me like a member of their family, and I feel privileged to share in the life God has given them in their rain forest home. We have shared many happy, and sad, times together; harvest celebrations, births, initiation rites, floods, epidemics, deaths.

Often, in the early days, when Juliet's gas supply ran low, and we had to wait for another load of fuel drums to arrive by river, I'd come by canoe and spend the waiting time with my new friends. We'd work on the landing strip for Juliet, and plant the new seeds, the new fruit trees, that I brought from Brazil. It was all good fun with my new friends. We would laugh and joke, and tease, and just enjoy being together.

Everyone in the tribe, from the youngest to the oldest, worked to clear enough jungle for Juliet to land near their maloca. Using only the machetes I brought from Brazil, stone axes, and brute strength to fell the huge jungle trees, it took almost a year to clear 700 meters of jungle. When Juliet and I made our first landing on their strip it was cause for a grand celebration.

They invited the neighboring tribes, and we flew in a large stuffed pig roasted in the bakery oven in Leticia. How good it was to see them so happy, so proud of their accomplishment.

Now my friend lies dying, and it is too late for medicine to help him. He stirs from the coma as I stand beside his hammock, holding his cold hands. He softly asks me to speak of dying.

I find the words in his tongue to reassure him that our Creator Spirit is in all that He creates, therefore He can never leave us. That dying in this world is going to live with "the Spirit who created the sky" for He loves us eternally.

I watch a tear slowly run down his cheek into a crevice at the corner of his mouth as he tries to smile. Then he is gone, with the beginning smile still on his lips. I hear a sound like the flutter of wings.

It all seems so unfair. At the prime of his short life he is a victim of a white man's disease. A few weeks ago, some Brazilian wood cutters spent a week in their maloca, partaking of the tribe's warm hospitality.

The fury of the raging storm is muffled by the thatched roof and quiet grieving inside the communal house. Lighted by the glow from a single glob of sap burning on the center pole, the maloca is filled with dark and long shadows moving slowly as the people prepare the bodies of the dead, and comfort the sick.

I feel very down and out as I go from hammock to hammock, showing the shaman how to measure the medicine, and give the injections to those it can help.

What am I doing here, I wonder, if I can't help my friends? What does it matter, when they keep dying anyway? If I can't keep my closest friends from dying, how can I hope to help the many others just like them? And who will preserve their rain forest home when the indigenous people of Amazonas are all gone?

By daybreak the storm has passed and the sun comes up in a cloudless sky, shining brightly. After refueling, Juliet and I climb into the blue sky, and head for the next village, with medicine to help quell the epidemic.

A thought crosses my mind. Many are dying, many are suffering, but some are living, with hope, because our spiritual journey brought us here to Amazonas. "Thank you, God."

CHAPTER 14

Juliet Charlie To The Amazon Headwaters
Year 1969   Age 38

"To live and fly in Amazonas requires a joyful heart, eyes open to the natural beauty all around, and an expansive soul to absorb it all."

It's a normal day of flying over the Amazon jungle. As normal as any day is when you're flying over the largest rain forest on earth, serving the most primitive people on earth, who love their jungle home as much as I love flying.

Juliet and I took-off at 0630, made four landings at short tribal strips. No epidemics, no snakebite victims, no big problems. Just the routine life of a solo jungle pilot.

On the last leg of a nine-hour flying day, our High Frequency radio crackles to life.

"Uno dos Juliet Charlie, Yarinacocha. Cambio."

It's a strong signal, for having traveled over hundreds of miles.

"Buenas tardes, Yarinacocha, Juliet Charlie. Siga."

The radio operator from the missionary base near the Rio Ucayali in the Peruvian area of Amazonas continues in English.

"Juliet Charlie, Yarina. I thought you might be interested in the latest news. I was on the short-wave HAM band last night talking with some friends in the States. They told me that man has landed on the moon.

"Yep, just like President Kennedy said, 'before this decade is out, we will send man to land on the moon.' I didn't hear when they actually got there, but they did land on the moon safely. And they're still up there, walking around on the moon. How about that?"

"Yarina, Juliet C. WOW! That's wonderful news! Yes, it means a lot to me. Whenever you hear more, please pass it on. Thank you, my friend. Juliet Charlie bye."

Suddenly a ho-hum day becomes spectacular. Flying over the rainforest, thinking of man landing on the moon is thrilling. Of course I'd give most anything to be on the moon with them right now, but I'm happy flying here in the jungle.

Juliet Charlie To The Amazon Headwaters

For my fellow pilots who have just become the first human beings to land on another celestial body, I am elated. Surely they know how very blessed they are to have the privilege of flying in space.

They can look out upon our blue planet and see how truly beautiful Earth really is. And they can look farther out and see the stars and galaxies ever so clearly, without interference of clouds or atmosphere. They can even watch the earthrise, just as we earthlings watch the sunrise and the moonrise.

Celebrating with some victory rolls over the jungle would be fun but Juliet isn't built for inverted flight. We settle for some milder fun and head for a playground of towering cumulus clouds.

After rejoicing with the clouds awhile, we spiral down under one cloud producing a little rain shower, for a free airplane wash. Then we chase the rainbow along the tree tops, celebrating life with the brightly colored toucans and parrots.

One of the many joys of jungle flying is the solitude, that feeling of complete aloneness. There are few places where a person can be totally alone, without any other humans around. The sky is one of them, especially the Amazon sky.

Juliet Charlie To The
Amazon Headwaters

We fly for hours, for hundreds of miles, and never see any sign of human habitation. Amazonas is the place to be for the "loner," especially the solo pilot.

Flying is full of fun, and to fly above the jungle of Amazonas is the most fun of all. We have the whole wide sky all to ourselves, to soar freely, to sway, to swing, to float on cushions of air so soft, so light, so fine, that they are invisible.

I fly simply because not to fly would be unthinkable. It's what I was put on this earth to do.

Juliet is my magic carpet and the Amazonas sky is our home. To play among her clouds, to explore her rivers, to fly where no one has ever flown before, is a special privilege known by few.

What a joy it is to have this gift of flight here in Amazonas! To see this land of superlatives from a condor's eye view. To look down upon her canopy, watch her rivers curl through endless treetops of every shade of green imaginable. To hear her heartbeat in the thunder, watch the rain feeding her trees and rivers. I wish I were a poet so I could share the beauty, the joy of flying in Amazonas, with words that touch the soul.

This huge rain forest is a miracle of God's creation, dating back to the time of the dinosaurs, 100 million years ago. Yet each day thousands of her acres are bulldozed, burned, destroyed.

Juliet Charlie To The
Amazon Headwaters

Part of nine countries, scarred by governments and large companies wanting to steal her natural resources, the jungles of Amazonas resists intrusions by unknowing and uncaring man intent on destroying her delicate natural balance.

Amazonas is by far the richest habitat left on earth, home to over half of the world's species of animal and plant life. This is the largest gene bank our world possesses, yet it could all disappear in our lifetime.

Unselfishly, Amazonas gives freely of her fruits, while begging that her trees not be destroyed. She nourishes her plants, vines, trees, rivers, with fresh water she makes from her own skies. Then freely gives of her overabundance to the world's oceans, providing twenty percent of the fresh water in the world.

The oxygen produced by her trees purifies the air we all breathe. The minerals, herbs, medicines within her reaches might well cure every illness known to man. If we would only care for her, taking of her fruits, not her heart and soul. She is like a mother to us all, nurturing us with her love, asking nothing in return but our caring love.

From Amazonas I receive inspiration and strength. The sheer exhilaration of flying in her skies is forever new. Every day she teaches me something new, shows me another thing of beauty, carries us gently in her skies.

Juliet Charlie To The Amazon Headwaters

Often Juliet and I crawl out from under a blanket of fog in the early morning and watch from above as the heat of the rising sun draws long silky wisps of water vapor curling up through her trees like smoke. Soon the fog blanket begins breaking up, like a quilt being shaken loose of it's cotton batting. Sometimes we play tag with these little "cotton ball" clouds, but usually we wait until they rise a couple of thousand feet. Now they have flat bottoms and billowing, towering tops.

Playing among her clouds is pure delight. We soar through endless valleys of clouds, curving, swerving, along sunlit corridors between walls of dazzling white closing in. Climbing, climbing, we top the mountain tops of boiling froth. Then plunge back down the other side to another playground of pristine whiteness. A playground ever changing, that never was before, never will be again, made only to enjoy this very second. We must seize the fun now, the splendor, at this very instant, or miss it forever. The joy of flying in her skies keeps me young in heart.

There are names for all these clouds: stratus, alto cumulus, cumulonimbus. But Amazonas has her own way with clouds. They are not formed by wind patterns, fronts, or jet streams, but in her very heart, a closed environmental system. That is why when one part of her jungle is destroyed, the hurt is felt in all the other parts. For all are interrelated, and need each other to keep alive and growing. She is empathetic, and fragile, the same as we are.

By late afternoon Amazonas is getting ready to nourish her family, and doesn't like to be disturbed. Her skies start turning dark, angry, violent, to ward off any unknowing intruders.

She gathers her towering clouds into gigantic thunderstorms, extending upwards to earth's stratosphere, above 60,000 feet. Then she sweeps them across her jungle, scattering seedpods for rebirth, leaves for mulch. And water, water, everywhere to nourish the intense growing cycle. We keep our distance at this time, filled with awe at the power of her might.

Sometimes I wonder how I've survived these six years as a jungle pilot. Certainly it hasn't been by skill, but by the grace of God, for there are many ways to kill yourself flying in Amazonas. One is to intrude into one of her late afternoon storms, after she has given you fair warning.

The storms pack the fury to freeze you instantly as the violent currents push your craft up, up, thousands of feet in seconds to the hail factory. There, what is left of your frail craft will be broken and ground into tiny bits and pieces, and spewed out into the icy stratosphere twelve miles above earth.

Or you might hit a downburst, which could tear you and your craft apart in a split second, spitting you out as so many broken toothpicks among the trees.

Another way for a pilot to die in the jungle is to get lost. You must make your own maps, know where you are at all times with only an occasional river to guide you. And unless you know exactly where the few short landing strips are located, hiding among the trees, it's best not to venture aloft over Amazonas.

The worst nightmare for a jungle pilot is to run out of daylight. The sun sets fast on the equator. There is no twilight. Once the sun is below the horizon, total blackness envelopes the entire jungle as quickly as if a room-darkening window shade has been pulled down.

Most pilots are optimists, and keep thinking "just a few more minutes and I'll find that strip." It is far better to purposely land in the tree tops before nightfall than fly on into darkness over Amazonas. If you have the fuel, you may fly on for hours, but you will not live to see another sunrise.

There is nowhere to land. No lights anywhere to show a maloca, a landing strip, or even a river. Nowhere to go. No navigation aids to guide you. No one to hear your plea for help. No radio station to tell a stranger your last words.

Juliet Charlie To The Amazon Headwaters

There is not a lighted airport anywhere, unless you can fly for hundreds of miles, and cross 20,000 foot Andean peaks. Nothing but deep blackness over your entire world. It is far better to take the one-in-a-thousand chance of surviving a crash landing in jungle treetops in the last rays of sunlight, than fly on into darkness over jungle. For you are only postponing the inevitable, oblivion.

There are simpler ways for a pilot to die in the jungle. A momentary power interruption, just a hiccup in the engine from dirty fuel, on take-off from a short strip will put you into the trees. A broken brake line on a short strip landing will do the same.

Amazonas is my home now. I love the challenge of flying in her skies, and am content to live in the isolation of her vastness. This is where my friends are.

The rain forest is breathtakingly beautiful and full of excitement. It's a magical place. You can feel the soul of Amazonas, her timelessness, in the majesty of her skies.

This wonderful land of contrasts with the mightiest rivers, the largest trees, is also home to the smallest tree frog, less than an inch long. And the tiniest bird, a "bee" hummingbird no bigger than it's namesake. The giant sloths, jaguars, condors, tapirs, capybaras, and giant otters of the world call

Amazonas home as well, providing an endless source of fascination.

There are over 200 kinds of mosquitos in this rain forest, but they never tasted malaria-tainted blood until the white man came. Then shamans found a treatment for malaria in the bark of the cinchona tree, quinine, which has saved millions of lives throughout the world.

To live and fly in Amazonas requires a joyful heart, eyes open to the natural beauty all around, and an expansive soul to absorb it all. Once you have lived in the heart of Amazonas and flown in her skies, you will never be the same again.

Juliet is my friend, my helper, my airplane. Most of all she is a source of hope, caring, aid, love, for those who live in the isolation of Amazonas. She has flown her heart out in this jungle, serving her friends. She is a legend in Amazonas.

I've changed her worn-out engines three times. She's always ready to go, hurting or not, and has well earned her retirement. But I keep patching her up, hoping she'll last one more year. Because to part with her would be like cutting off my right arm, or selling my only child.

Juliet came to Amazonas with me, a frisky little bird, and we learned together. Caring for people, not things, is what our work is all about, but I must admit a certain fondness for her. When I fly all day with her, tend my sick friends in her, eat in her, sleep in her, pray in her, she becomes a real part of me.

She is my home, my chapel, my magic carpet. We have shared the most gorgeous sights in this land of wonders, and suffered through the worst of storms. Many are the nights I have listened to the jungle rain beat down on her metal wings like billions of BBs, while she cradled me in her dry cabin. In the air, or on the ground, she has never let me down. Not once.

Juliet knows her way around this overwhelming jungle almost by heart, and today we're on our way to the headwaters area of Amazonas. Here is where it all begins when the water-laden storms of the jungle drop their heavy burdens on the eastern slope of the Andes as they rise to cross the high mountains, and float out over the Pacific Ocean.

Torrents of rain come crashing down the steep Andean slopes, running from the foothills into the creeks that surge through the jungle, hidden under the trees.

Rapidly gaining strength, they become rivers snaking among the trees, growing every mile, until the jungle's thick canopy can no longer hide them. Taking strength from the sun, the hundreds of rivers crash through the massive foliage, often cutting new paths among the trees, leaving the old river beds to become closed-end lakes, filling with each new rain.

Juliet Charlie To The
Amazon Headwaters

During a jungle rain, the rivers can rise twenty or thirty feet overnight, taking large trees with them in their rush to their mother, the Rio Amazonas. At the joining of her waters the unique brown and black colors of her tributaries can be seen for forty miles downriver, until the mighty river absorbs all.

With a thousand miles yet to go, the Rio Amazonas spans four to six miles across, almost further than the eye can see. Warm as blood, her eddies create whirlpools that toss broken trees around like match sticks. She is stained with jungle mud and organic matter, wild but mute.

Rushing, growing, she claws island-size chunks of land from her banks, as she sweeps everything in her path towards the other sea, the Atlantic Ocean. Her mouth spans 200 miles across and contributes one-fifth of the world's fresh water to sweeten the oceans of the world.

We don't often fly this far up in the headwaters. The indigenous people living in this hidden place are hard to reach.

Their forefathers were beaten and starved to death by rubber hunters during the boom days, when the white men took advantage of their hospitality to enslave them. Every day they were forced to run through the jungle tapping the rubber trees in exchange for food. Each day their quota of latex was increased, while their food supplies were decreased, until they died of starvation or physical exhaustion, whichever came first.

When the seeds of the Amazon rubber tree were planted in Malaysia and the boom ended in South America, the few indigenous people left in this area, who could muster the strength, made their way upriver. They were helped by people from other tribes who had escaped earlier, giving them dugout canoes, paddles, cassava for the journey.

This group traveled as far upriver as they could paddle, then turned up a creek, and pulled the dugouts by vines until they could go no farther. There they settled, in this headwaters area, building one communal maloca to shelter the remnants of their tribe. Living every day in fear of the white man, and the evil spirits.

Their home is dead ahead. A lone maloca half hidden by the trees. We make a low pass to check the rough strip. It looks O.K.

Sharp pull up, 90 degree turn.

Another 90 to downwind, slow her down.

Gear down, locked, pressure up.

Not too low, or the trees will block our view of the strip.

Turn onto base, partial flaps.

Final approach now, line her up.

Full flaps, props forward, fuel boosts on.

Slow her down ... more.

Low, slow, with power, hanging on the props.
Add some power, just above the tree tops.
Clear the last 200 footer, cut the power.
Dive for the end of the strip.
Wait until she's right over the end.
Flare, level off, nose up.
Instant stall.
PLOP, we're down.
Riding the roller coaster.
Stay on the rudders.
Hold her yoke back, all the way.
Lay on the brakes.

We skid to a stop in front of the primitive people with painted bodies and faces. They're shaking their blowguns and spears at us, as they surround Juliet and me.

CHAPTER 15

Shamans Fly To The Moon
Year 1969   Age 38

*"When we see the beauty of little things,
we become aware of the splendor all around us."*

Being surrounded by naked hunters with painted bodies and faces, shaking their spears and blowguns at us, would have scared the daylights out of me in times past. But these are our friends, and this is their way of welcoming us.

As soon as I shut down Juliet's engines and open her door, they drop their hunting tools and run towards us with open arms, each wanting a hug. We laugh, and tease, and tell each other how happy we are to be together again.

After everyone is greeted and hugged, it's time to take care of Juliet, turning her around to line her up for an early take-off tomorrow, refueling, and buttoning her down for the night.

On their narrow strip they know the turning procedure well. We lift up the youngest kids to sit on the flat part of Juliet's tail, like so many sandbags. Their combined weight brings her tail down, lifting her nose wheel off the ground like a seesaw.

Amid squeals and laughter we take the youngsters "flying" as we gently push six-thousand-pound Juliet around in a half circle, with her nose wheel up in the air. When we lift each "sandbag" kid off the tail, her nose gently returns to earth. Push her back to the end of the strip, and she's lined up for tomorrow's take-off.

Refueling in the jungle is by bucket, five gallons at a time. The 100 octane avgas is poured through filters, and sometimes an old t-shirt. They both serve well in removing the dirt and rust from the fifty-gallon fuel storage drums. Sometimes I also use a chamois to strain out the water that has accumulated in the metal drums from condensation.

We try to keep the fuel drums filled at each tribal strip with periodic fuel runs when there is time. Each run takes most of the day and we carry 400 gallons, 200 in the wings, and 200 in four drums strapped down in Juliet's cabin. Since each full drum weighs over 300 pounds, I have to siphon the precious fuel out of the cabin drums before removing them.

After years of practice, I've found that there is no easy way to refuel Juliet when I'm alone in the jungle. It is dreary, hard, exhausting work. First I have to fill the five-gallon bucket from the heavy drum and lift it up to sit on Juliet's high wing. Then I climb up onto the wing, pour it into her tank, and climb back down. Repeating every five gallons, or about forty times to top off her tanks.

Refueling often takes half the day when I'm alone. Longer, when it's raining, since I have to keep the bucket, drum and wing tank openings covered with ponchos. With lots of eager hands and strong backs helping today, it goes fast, and Juliet is soon topped off.

The youngsters carry her control locks from aileron to rudder to stabilizer, helping me install them to keep any errant wind in the night from awakening the Bird. That's what our indigenous friends call her, in their language.

She has many names, in many tongues. In Spanish she's usually called Amiga (friend) or La Pajarita (little bird). I call her Juliet, short for her call sign, One-Two-Juliet-Charlie.

The pitot tube cover is put on last, so insects won't nest in her airspeed indicator. No need to lock her doors, everyone around here loves her. Now Juliet's tucked in for her well-earned rest.

The Chief knows where I stow my hammock and has removed it from under the rear seat. The people are waiting for me to accompany them to their maloca, where they live, eat, and sleep under one large palm-thatched roof. When I say I have something important to tell them, they anxiously gather around Juliet. The Chief helps me tie my hammock under her left wing, landing gear to wingtip.

Seated in my hammock under her wing, with our friends gathered around, I look for the moon. It's just visible in the clearing, rising above the tree tops. I begin speaking slowly, in their language.

"Man has flown higher in the sky than ever before. Higher even than the strongest bird. Just a few days ago, man landed on the moon." Pointing at the moon now, I continue. "And they are still up there, walking around on the moon."

Sitting back in my hammock I wait for their excited reaction. But they merely look around, a little bewildered, stealing glances at each other, smiling, like maybe I'm teasing them. They like to tease, and are always coming up with new ways to tease me. That's one of the many things that endear them to me. That, and knowing that they are really as shy as I am.

Maybe I'm using the wrong words in their tongue, and they don't understand what I'm trying to say. I try again.

"Man has indeed flown to the moon. For the first time ever, man is actually walking around on another land in the sky. The moon, right there, (pointing) that we're looking at."

They look at the moon, back to me. They look at their chief, their shaman, still bewildered. They don't seem to understand the importance of man landing on the moon. They begin to talk about the new seeds and fruit trees we have brought them, the parrots they have shot with their blowguns for their daily meal.

Now I'm confused by their total lack of interest in this momentous news. Seeing this, the chief nods to one of the young shamans-in-training, who gently explains.

"Even the youngest among us knows that one of our shaman ancestors, Birdman, flew to the moon many times. He told our forefathers all about it, that the moon is a good spirit, feminine, and gives her light to us at night to protect us from harm."

Now I understand their lack of interest in my "news." A smile creeps across my face as I jump up from my hammock and hug the young shaman. They all laugh, and start talking excitedly about the good visit we will have in their maloca tonight.

Amid moans and groans, I have to explain that I need to be alone tonight, look at the moon, sleep with the Bird. They're disappointed, but they understand. I promise to come to their maloca at daybreak, so we can have a good visit then.

They want to build a fire for us, "to keep the evil spirits, and the night animals, away." With thanks I tell them to save their precious dry firewood for cooking. Trusting the moon spirit to watch over us, they rush to the safety of their maloca before night falls.

What gentle, loving people they are, whose very culture teaches them to welcome all strangers, feed them, care for them. Even when the strangers mistreat them. Even when they don't have enough food for themselves.

Many times my indigenous friends insist that I eat their last piece of meat, or cassava, while they go hungry. Often I find a friend huddled on the cold ground around the final embers of the cooking fire late at night, because he has insisted that I sleep in his dry hammock when mine is still wet from the rain. To refuse is to deny them the pleasure of sharing. To not accept their generosity is considered an insult in their communal society.

During the past six years I have experienced some of the hardest, most difficult flying of my life. Flying every day over the largest jungle in the world, with no aeronautical charts, no radio reports, no navigation aids, no weather forecasts, no airports, no electricity, no refueling facilities, is certainly a challenge. Especially in the wildest weather on earth.

My time here in Amazonas has also been the most rewarding of my life. It all began in the sky with God, on a Jamaican beach with God. Having received so much, I wanted to share those gifts.

When my spiritual journey brought me to Amazonas to serve the indigenous people, I didn't think I had the fortitude to live in this overpowering land. The warmth of the indigenous people who welcomed me with true hospitality melted those doubts.

When we first arrived in Amazonas I wasn't sure I had the courage to fly over this enormous jungle. After six years of flying in Amazonas skies, and living with her people, now I'm not sure I would have the courage to leave.

Every day I learn from these primitive people who befriend me. All day, every day, they are out in the jungle searching for food to survive one more day. And they happily share their meager monkey or parrot meat with me, who flies in the comfort of Juliet all day.

The medicines we bring, mostly antibiotics, vaccines, and anti-venom, I give to their shamans, and show them how to use them. They teach me about medicines the jungle yields to help their people.

My new friends also teach me about caring for each other, sharing, living together with gentleness and love when all you have is each other. I've learned how important it is to have people like them in my life.

We learn together. We find that the little joys of everyday life more than make up for the big disappointments of life. From the youngest to the oldest, they take delight in showing me the special beauty of their jungle home. Nowhere else on earth is there such a diversity of all forms of life as in this rain forest.

To those who have nothing, everything is a gift. The sunrise, the soft song of a bird, a tiny tree frog with a big voice, announcing the rain. A butterfly flitting it's iridescent wings among the jungle vines. a beetle dressed in bright florescent green. These, and all of life, are gifts to be received with joy and gratitude. When we see the beauty of little things, we become aware of the splendor all around us. In the things that are created, we see the love of the Creator.

We know that He who created all things, also made each of us. We see his love in each other, in the children, the jungle, the sky, the rain. And in the flowers, the birds, the insects, cassava. We know that his love for all his creation is endless.

My indigenous friends live in a bigger world than many of us. The rivers, the trees of their jungle home, the sky, the sun, the moon, the stars, the universe, are always on their minds. They may live together under one thatched roof and have to search for food each day, but they live in a magnificent universe to which they are very sensitive. They understand that the inner life of the soul depends on the outer world of nature.

Each tribe builds one palm-thatched maloca to live in. Each man takes one wife, with the blessing of their chief and their shaman. In tribal communal living under one roof, intimate moments are reserved for the privacy of the jungle during the day. Most families are grateful to have one or two children still living, since most die in their early years.

The women and children spend all day in the planting field, cultivating their main crop, cassava, a large tuberous root. It is the mainstay of their diet, filling their stomachs when there is nothing else to eat, and keeping the children from crying with hunger pains. But there is not a gram of protein in it, it's pure starch. With all the cassava they can eat, many still die of malnutrition when the men cannot find meat in the jungle.

To prepare the cassava the women grate the tuber on a piece of tree trunk into which they have embedded tiny sharpened pebbles. The resulting mash is then put into a six-foot long narrow strainer which is woven of palm fronds, much like the old Chinese finger catcher. It hangs on a pole in the maloca, and as the bottom end is pulled, the strainer becomes more narrow, squeezing out the juice, which runs down the sides. They have to make sure to get all the juice out, for this is not the sweet cassava that tapioca comes from. It is bitter cassava, and its juice is cyanide.

It is a terrible thing to watch a toddler die because he sticks his fingers in his mouth after they have been in the cassava juice on the dirt floor of the maloca. There is no antidote for cyanide poison.

All day, every day, the men run through the jungle hunting with bow and arrow, spears, or blowguns and darts they make from jungle reeds. A good day's hunt will net a few scrawny monkeys, or a rodent or two, to feed the entire tribe.

Fish is feast or famine, coming through the small creeks only twice a year, as they migrate with water levels. Ants and termites are another twice a year delicacy when they take to the air in their mating ritual.

By late afternoon everyone is back home in the maloca, and heads down to the creek to bathe, the men at one spot, the women and children at another.

Before dark, all are safely back in the maloca, for no one ventures forth into the jungle after sunset. Night time in the jungle belongs to the jaguars, ocelots, giant sloths, panthers, vampire bats, capybara, and other nocturnal creatures.

Evening is the time for socializing, animated talk is heard in all quarters of the maloca. The meat, if any, and the cassava, are cooked and shared by all. By eight or nine in the evening it's beginning to get quiet in the maloca as palm-string hammocks are lowered from the roof poles, and tied for the night's rest.

The young children sleep with their mothers in hammocks at one end of the maloca, the men and older boys tie their hammocks at the other end. They sleep until about four or five in the morning, when the struggle to survive another day begins anew.

With over 400 inches of rain a year it's hard to find nourishing crops that will grow in the jungle, but I keep trying. This time I've brought some long bean seeds from Brazil, and papaya seedlings from Bolivia. Hopefully they will grow here and improve their protein-poor diet, making life a little easier for these gentle people.

No one knows how many indigenous tribes there are today, but there are far fewer than there were. In the late 1400s more people were living in the Americas, 100 million, than in all of Europe, 80 million. Over ninety percent of America's indigenous people were killed by oppression and disease after Colombus discovered the "new world." It was only "new" to the Europeans. Tens of millions of Americans died, entire cultures, nations, religions vanished. It was one of the world's worse catastrophes.

True to their culture, the indigenous people welcomed Columbus and those who followed him, with true hospitality. They gave the foreigners shelter, food, and offered them gifts of whatever they had. The white men marveled at the shiny gold ornaments the natives sometimes wore, and soon began killing their hosts, and destroying their most sacred places in order to steal their gold ornaments.

The indigenous people could never understand why their people were killed, and their beautiful works of art melted down into golden rocks. To them the value of the shiny yellow substance was in the art forms their artisans crafted, not the material itself.

Gold is not the only reason the indigenous people are killed. It's still going on today, although on a lesser scale. Now they are killed for their jungle land, or for the exotic hardwoods of their rain forest home. Or just because some people think they are like animals, without souls, to be hunted down and killed just for sport.

These primitive people are said to be ignorant, backwards, stupid, when, in truth, they are brilliant naturalists. They have learned to use the plants and animals of the jungle while maintaining the diversity of their rain forest home. Indeed they have been the true preservers of this jungle for thousands of years.

To those intent on robbing Amazonas of her natural resources, my friends are considered a nuisance, a pest to be done away with, the same as the big jungle cats, jaguars, panthers, and ocelots. Sometimes bounties are placed on their heads.

With all these atrocities visited upon them, it's a wonder they still welcome strangers. But they do, with true hospitality, for they are kind, gentle, peaceful people. They are precious human beings in whom God delights in showing his love. We will miss so much without them.

Of all the endangered species in the world today, the most endangered of all, is our very own. Primitive man is only heartbeats away from extinction. Less than six percent of the original tribes survive today.

It's getting dark now, and I can see the smoke rising through the thatch of their maloca in the moonlight. They're cooking their parrots and cassava for everyone to share in their one meal of the day.

Alone now, I climb up on top of Juliet's high wing, and sit there a long time. Looking across the tree tops at the almost full moon, I listen to the night sounds of the jungle all around us. It's one of those magical nights, clear, sparkling, luminous.

Six years, that's how long it's been, since I walked out of that Congressional Hearing room on Capitol Hill, knowing that I would not be allowed to fly in space, that I had wasted three years of my life preparing to be an astronaut. The year was 1963, and my country, my culture, was not ready to allow a woman to fly in space.

Those three years had been the most difficult of my professional life. Not the astronaut tests, or the flying. But the press interviews, television appearances, speeches, that were required of me as a NASA consultant. Having to answer personal questions, revealing my most private thoughts was almost more than I could bear.

As with many Congressional Hearings, a lot was said, but nothing ever done about including women pilots in our nation's space program. A few months later in 1963, Russia astounded the world by sending the first woman into space, a factory worker named Valentina Tereshkova.*

(*Note: Twenty years later an American woman rode into space, Sally Ride, a physicist, in 1983. Thirty-two years later, USAF Colonel Eileen Collins became the first American woman pilot to fly in space, in 1995.)

The glow of the moon reflecting on the wing gives me that marvelous sense of being in perfect harmony with the universe. From the sky, Juliet and I may look like a speck on earth's floor, surrounded by jungle, but we're a part of the marvelous whole.

Yes, I wish I were on the moon with my fellow pilots, exploring another celestial body. How I would love to see our beautiful blue planet Earth floating in the blackness of space. And see the stars and galaxies in their true brilliance, without the filter of our atmosphere. But I'm happy flying here in Amazonas, serving my brethren. "Contenta, Señor, contenta, (I am happy, Lord, happy.")

The moon is higher now, spreading her light across the jungle tree tops. The world is still as the moonlight quiets my heart. I'm caught up in the magical glow, sitting cross-legged on the top of Juliet's wing, in the middle of the rain forest. I begin to address our astronauts on the moon.

"Congratulations, fellow pilots. Your amazing flight brings joy to my heart. You are fulfilling my deepest dream."

The growl of a jaguar in the distance, the rustling of small, scared animals, interrupts my thoughts for a minute. Then I return to thinking of our astronauts on the moon.

"Look deep into your souls, search the wonders of the universe, don't forget a single thing. You are exploring the depth of our souls, for that which is infinite in us lives in the sky. Come back and tell us what we long to hear, for we need to see what you are seeing, to hear of the wonders that only your eyes have seen. Vaya con Dios, my brothers."

For hours I sit on Juliet's wing in the silvery light of the moon, looking, listening, taking in all the beauty of the moment. Yes, I still yearn to fly in space, it's the only thing that could possibly take me away from my friends here. But I would always return to my jungle friends, for I have finally found a home, beneath the moon.

After awhile I stand up, stretch the kinks out. That's when I decide to do a little dance in the light of the moon, from wingtip to wingtip. I may look silly, dancing alone in the moonlight, on top of an airplane wing, in the middle of the jungle. But it feels good. Only God is watching, and I think he's smiling.

Patting Juliet as I climb down to the jungle floor, I slip into my damp hammock still tied under her left wing, cover up with an old mosquito net, and sleep like a baby, the rest of the night that man walked on the moon.

Shamans Fly To The Moon

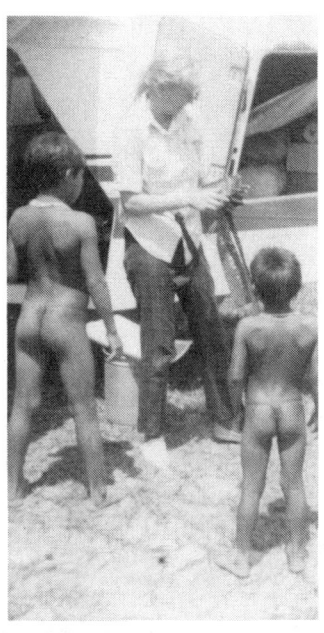

Index

A Andes, 74, 165, 166
Argentina, 124
Awards, 6, 7
B B-17, 77-102
Bahamas, 160, 161
Barranquilla, 59, 60
C Cali, 60-63
Carolyn, 19-21, 93
Cartagena, 163
Clouds, 15-17, 29, 198
Coffey, Ivy 131-132
Cub, 5, 9-17, 26-29
D DC-3, 32, 101, 102
E Earhart, Amelia 164
F
G Glenn, John, 6, 154, 154
Greenland, 87-96
Guayaquil, 65-73
H
I
J Jamaica, 57-58, 105-122, 154
K

L Leticia, 168, 169
Llanos, 166, 167
London, 124
M Magdalena, 60, 164
Malacca, 127
Moon, 184, 211, 212
N NASA, 6, 140-149, 159
New York, 123
O
P Paris, 77, 98-100, 124, 159
Ponca City, 92
Q
R
S
T Tereshkova, Valentina, 150, 210
U Thaden, Louise 164
V
W WACO, 5, 22, 23
Webb, Coby, 78-102
X, Y, Z